AFRICAN POP

Goodtime Kings

BY BILLY BERGMAN

BLANDFORD PRESS
POOLE • DORSET

First published in the U.K. 1985
by Blandford Press
Link House, West Street,
Poole, Dorset, BH15 1LL

A QUARTO BOOK
Copyright © 1985 by Quarto Marketing Ltd.

British Library Cataloguing in Publication Data

Bergman, William
    African pop: goodtime kings—(The
Planet rock series: 3)
    1. Music, Popular (Songs, etc.)—Africa—
History and criticism
    I. Title   II. Series
    780'.42'0904   ML3505.A3
ISBN: 0-7137-1551-0

AFRICAN POP: Goodtime Kings
was prepared and produced by
Quarto Marketing Ltd.
15 West 26th Street, New York, N.Y. 10010

Editor: Karla Olson
Cover and book design: Rod Gonzalez
Photo Research: Susan M. Duane

Typeset by BPE Graphics, Inc.
Printed and bound in the United States by
The Maple-Vail Group

Cover photo by Chris Walter/Retna Ltd.

ACKNOWLEDGMENTS

Special thanks to Bob George of Blackmarket Records, New York City, for making his extensive research material, including interviews, recordings, contacts, and literature, available for use in this project; for contributing his experience on tour with Ebenezer Obey; and for his advice on the discographies. Additional grateful thanks to all those who provided information, acted as guides, and helped with arrangements in the U.S., Europe, and West Africa, including: Dmitri Samaras, Andrea Bergman, Glaou Sebo Blaise, Ernest Nzekio, Idriss and Martine Diabate, Paul Wassaba, Akin Medeiros, Sigi Yebovi, Nelson Tackie, Charles E.D. Williams, Kanga and Dominique, Tom Johnson, Annetta Hanna, Corinne LaBalme, Jean-Marie Salaun, Jean-Pierre Frescaline, Emmanuel Bovet, John Baskin, Duma Ndlovu, Dr. George Nwagei, Jak Kilby, Traore Richard, Bill Logan, and Gene Santoro. And thanks to editor Karla Olson for her patience and assistance.

A F R I C A

MEDITERRANEAN SEA

TUNISIA

MOROCCO

ALGERIA

LIBYA

EGYPT

RED SEA

MAURITANIA

MALI

NIGER

CHAD

SUDAN

DJIBOUTI

SENEGAL

GAMBIA

GUINEA-BISSAU

GUINEA

UPPER VOLTA

SIERRA LEONE

IVORY COAST

NIGERIA

CENTRAL AFRICAN REPUBLIC

ETHIOPIA

SOMALIA

LIBERIA

GHANA

TOGO

BENIN

CAMEROON

EQ. GUINEA

GABON

PEOPLES REPUBLIC OF THE CONGO

ZAIRE

UGANDA

KENYA

RWANDA

BURUNDI

TANZANIA

INDIAN OCEAN

MALAWI

MOZAMBIQUE

ATLANTIC OCEAN

N

ANGOLA

ZAMBIA

ZIMBABWE

NAMIBIA

BOTSWANA

SWAZILAND

SOUTH AFRICA

LESOTHO

The specific countries whose music is examined in this book are indicated by solid grey; the vast area south of the Sahara Desert throughout which this music is influential is indicated by grey dots.

CONTENTS

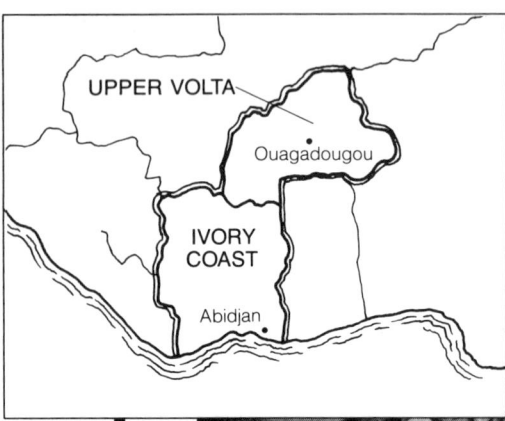

UPPER VOLTA

Ouagadougou

IVORY
COAST

Abidjan

Idriss Diabate

WARBA

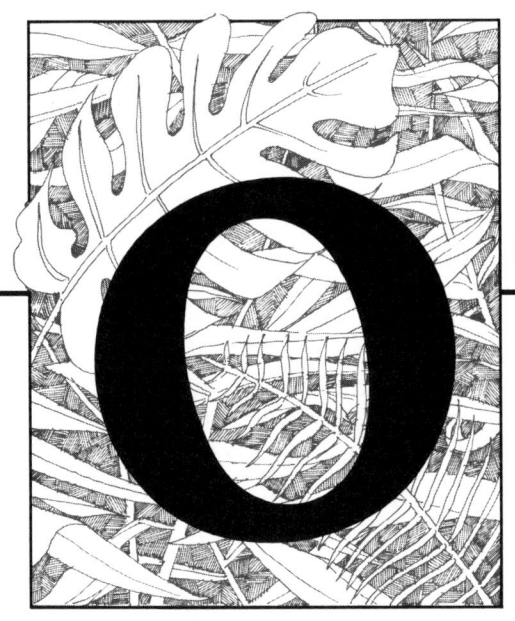

Chapter · One

Once-distant African drums have been coming closer and closer and getting louder and louder in recent years. The ominous beating became friendlier, if not less exotic, with the 50s release of Olatunji's Yoruba *Drums of Passion* album. Then a 1967 field recording of drummers from Burundi gained worldwide popularity through the 70s, and without the drummers' knowledge (according to music sleuth David Toop), the recording was released on various labels, was backup for Joni Mitchell in her 1975 *Hissing of Summer Lawns* album, was "discovered" in 1979 by British producer Malcolm McLaren as the musical gimmick of the group Bow Wow Wow, and was sold as a concept by McLaren to Adam Ant in 1980. In the 80s, other new wave groups began to put full-blown multipart rhythms into their music; most successful were Talking Heads. There have been new experimentalists, such as Steve Reich and Jon Hassell, who, inspired by African models, have made "percussion the dominant voice" in their ensembles, as Reich puts it. There's an increasing realization of the African roots in rock 'n' roll and rhythm 'n' blues, and the corresponding buildup of complicated rhythmic layers in dance music such as disco and hip hop.

Lately, there's a new awareness of African music in Europe and the United States. Routed through higher education and the international record business, Africans playing electric instruments have begun showing up in Paris, London, and even New York and Los Angeles. Paul McCartney spoke of a thriving pop music scene in Lagos, Nigeria, while recording his *Band on the Run* album there at the studio of Ginger Baker, ex-drummer of Cream. The Top Forty disco machine allowed some African hits, such as Manu Dibango's

Alpha Blondy, the reggae singer from the Ivory Coast, as depicted on the wall of a dance hall on the outskirts of Abidjan.

1973 "Soul Makossa," to fly up the charts avoiding the pigeonhole of ethnic music. Fela Ransome (now Anikulapo) Kuti's pidgin protests avoided that same trap by fulfilling the wildest dreams of James Brown fans, with albums like *Expensive Shit* and *Zombie* finding their way to underground radio and hip record collections.

Then, pow!, Sunny Adé, Nigerian master guitarist, King, Minister of Enjoyment, and bandleader of the African Beats, was picked up by Island Records and, in 1983, sold out rock venues around the world. Rock fans found themselves dancing to massed talking drummers and percussive and slide guitarists, saying to themselves, "It sounds so much like rock and country, and so much like African music at the same time. I suppose it makes sense, if rock music has roots in Africa...."

But there's more than simple fusion going on south of the Sahara. Western listeners realized this when they couldn't figure out what was Afro and what was Cuban in the soukous music of Zairians Franco and Rochereau, or pin down the origin of their fast-picking electric guitars. And Westerners were confused and elated when Mandingo Mory Kante came to Paris and vocalized Arabic modes while exhorting them to dance with an amplified kora, a harp with a huge resonating bulb. Of course, a back-and-forth of musical ideas has been going on for centuries, maybe even millenia. East Africa and Indonesia probably traded xylophone sounds before recorded history; string instruments made their way down caravan routes from the north. More recently, Africans forced into slavery brought music with them to the New World. There, it combined with European music, creating dance and song forms that are not tied to any specific ethnic group or any specific ceremony, but encourage listeners to have a good time—"popular music." The resulting forms, such as rhumba, calypso, and rock, came back to Africa, with sailors and on the radio. This "popular music," smacking of something familiar but using new instruments and structures, fulfilled an awakening need in Africans, arising from an unfamiliar situation more and more Africans found themselves in after World War II—city living.

In African cities, as in the New World, members of different tribal groups came together and mixed, especially in the urban dance hall. And a new pan-ethnic celebration was created, a product of urban work schedules—Saturday Night. The new good time music was perfect for this occasion, and African musicians transformed it little by little to suit their feelings and rhythmic backgrounds, taking what they wanted from Western instrumentation, international hits, and pan-African fads. First identifiable as highlife, and sounding a lot like calypso, this music changed rapidly during the

Jak Kilby

A bus stops in a north Ghana town on its way to Accra.

50s as musicians began looking inward to their own, specific tribal rhythms. As a result, there is a rich variety of regional music today that is the African modern music, but also fulfills some of the roles of traditional music. Sunny Adé's juju music, for example, does this for the Yorubas; besides the Saturday night club celebrations, juju musicians are engaged for traditional occasions from a funeral to the installation ceremony of a village chief.

The image of a large amplified band with four or five electric guitarists playing at a village funeral may seem strange, but plucked instruments are as indigenous to Africa as drums are. There is a version of the plucked hand piano, in whose pentatonic lines the origins of modern African guitar styles can easily be recognized in nearly every region of Africa. It's called the mbira or kalimba in southern regions, and the likembe, ikenbe, sanza, sanzi, etc., farther north. With a tuning of do re mi sol la, sanzas have between five and thirty metal strips that are plucked to make the notes. There are bass as well as tenor and soprano sanzas, and they are often played in ensembles. As on rock guitars, impure or "dirty" pitches are often expressly created on the sanza with little pieces of metal attached to the strips so they buzz with every pluck.

The sanza and any of its relatives are held in high spiritual esteem in African culture and even find a place in creation legends. Francis Bebey, a Cameroonian musician and musicologist, relates this story told to him by a night watchman in Nairobi, Kenya: At first, there was nothing except Nyambe, the creator, and he was bored. His imagination told him to make a sanza. The first note he plucked separated light from darkness; the next note made a man. "Good," said Nyambe when he saw this person. "I needed you to listen to my sanza music. Listen." As Nyambe played, he and the first man were so enthralled by the music that they didn't notice that each note produced a man or a woman. When he stopped playing, much to their surprise, there was a world crowded with men and women of all races.

"As in most cases where the sound is produced by *plucking* the instrument," continues Bebey, "the use of the fingers establishes a privileged though intangible contact between man and the world beyond, and beyond that, between man and the general domain of the invisible." This thought could apply to the electric guitar as well—which is plucked in a comparable manner—and may explain why African musicians have been able to master the electric guitar so completely that they have transformed it for their own purposes, both pop and ceremonial.

Through the Africanization of musical ideas and technology from abroad, Africans have taken an important first step toward confronting the onslaught of influence from industrial nations. Disruptions caused by colonialism, international business, and misguided development programs may continue to cause rampant confusion and disaster, but the arts and entertainments may become a beachhead in the battle to transform imported Western ideas to make them usable in African culture. Soccer, for example, has blended as naturally into African identity as soccer balls have into batik patterns now used in traditional wraps and tailored shirts. Novelists such as Chinua Achebe have used the oral tale as the basis for a completely new form of novel. New forms of painting, using acrylics and motifs derived from razor blades and bicycle spokes, are cropping up all over; startling bas reliefs with traditional clashing patterns in Abidjan, the Ivory Coast, turn out to be made of thousands of matchsticks pasted together. "The alteration of African art as it meets white urban culture is sad for purists and symbolizes a political reality no one wants," says Denise Scott Brown, an architectural critic. "But it is probably the liveliest artistic reaction that has come out of southern Africa."

In music, appreciation of the new transformations has been long in coming, veiled by mourning and ranting over the destruction of traditional music styles due to Anglo-American cultural domination. As for musicologists, critic Bruno Nettl says, "They have only lately recognized that some of the most interesting and significant events in the recent history of world music result from the rapid growth, modernization, and Westernization of cities in the developing or recently developed nations outside Europe and North America." Cities are the cauldrons in which the chart-breaking new pop styles are brewing. They are the centers of hepped-up optimism in which soukous, highlife, kwela, and other uplifting or good time musics set the beat, and the courts of the good time royalty who are the stars of this music. But an easier entree into the complex world of modern African music can be gained at small, regional centers where international and pan-African fads meet regional rhythms.

One enters through a breach in a wall, the kind of wall that surrounds all the compounds that break up the great plains of Africa, defining the territory of a family, civic agency, school, or business. This particular wall surrounds a dance club. It's just higher than a tall man and is made of concrete blocks set lengthwise and crossed every few yards by columns of horizontal blocks. It is coated with the red dust that covers everything in the Sahel region south of the Sahara, a region that makes up the northern portion of most West African states and which is rapidly eroding to desert. On this Saturday night, a small community of people takes care of business in front of the breach. Young boys who have recently come to the city from surrounding villages arrange to guard the arriving motorbikes; women wrapped in cloth sit in front of small tables selling kola nuts and cigarettes set out in a bouquet or snacks stapled into plastic bags. The dry air is heavy with dust and lingering heat left over from midday, mingling with the smells of spicy food and open sewers bridged by walkways. The women collecting entry fees for the club keep company with friends, family, and prostitutes catching an early glimpse of potential clientele. Khaki-clad soldiers may be sitting around the entryway, too, depending on the regime of the moment; it's not clear whether they're on duty or just hanging out. Their rifles—a sampling from the history of arms, from pre-World War II carbines to automatic weapons with prosthetic shoulder butts—are loosely crooked in their elbows. Everyone at the entryway must be greeted with a hand squeeze and a solemn ça va or bonjour.

Through the breach, after a couple of turns, the club opens into a large courtyard, and the music fills out into layers of amplified sound bouncing off the walls. There is no roof (there are no stars, either, because of the dust) except for a covered pavilion in the center, its concrete floor packed with people dancing the heavy, off-

A wide variety of music is broadcast all over Africa. Somewhere in Mali, a young Marabout tunes in.

Ph. Cl. Mahaoudeau/Edimedia

beat jerk of reggae, their translucent dark skin taking on the green of the colored fluorescent light. The light is there by order of the latest government, which had closed all the nightclubs in a moral and anti-subversive fervor, allowing them to reopen only as illuminated people's dance halls, hoping the lights would prevent any objectionable goings-on. Even with the lights, clubs have recently been swept for prostitutes, and many innocent single women have been carted off to prison along with the bona fide working girls.

At the far end, under another shelter, is the band, pumping out their version of a recent reggae hit, "Cocody Rock" by Alpha Blondy of the Ivory Coast. The young singer parrots the English lyrics perfectly; the organ, set to the skating rink sound, woofs on the off-beat with the patent Jamaican accent. The fourteen-member ensemble creates a denser texture than in most reggae songs; this is a rough-hewn but powerful version of the original song. The band, the most popular one in Ouagadougou, Upper Volta (now called Burkina Faso—the name of the country was changed during the same coup that lit up the nightclubs), is called Desi et les Sympathiques. The bandleader, Traore Desiree (a.k.a. Desi), is one-half of the brass section, playing a brash alto sax. "I've been trying to get kids to learn sax and the other horns for the band," he says. "We even have one for them to play. But they all want to play guitar—most kids can play a little guitar and besides, it's the rock star image. So I had to learn sax myself. This is the first time I'm playing it at a club date." The reggae song fades out and stops. The dancers flee from the pavilion.

Bass, drums, and shakers begin a more complex rhythm. The musicians begin singing in More, a local language of the Ouagadougou area. Everyone rushes up to the pavilion, leaving a forest of empty, two-foot-tall green beer bottles behind on the tables. "It's a Warba!" someone explains as he joins the crowd. "That's our local rhythm." Even a civil service driver in the proper grey safari suit, who had refrained up to this point, joins the enthusiastic crowd. Facing the same direction, the dancers shake their shoulders and hips and advance slowly, en masse, around the dance floor. The electric guitars are playing the most basic chords of pop music—one and five—but they shift the jagged motifs in and out. The conga drummer abandons the repetitive, ornamental role he had played in the reggae song and becomes a soloist. The keyboard plays a pentatonic pattern as lilting as any played on a hand piano or balaphone (wooden xylophone). This is their village music, played with what is basically a large rock 'n' roll ensemble, and for the moment the dancers forget their Western clothing and let themselves slip back into their youth.

The music suddenly fades out. The magic spell is over, and the dancers quickly clear the floor again. A waitress in a t-shirt that says Le Club Canari, apparently the name of the place, comes and circles the plastic-covered table, greeting everyone with a humorless, limp handshake and a *bonjour.* She asks what is wanted and soon more large local beers appear, along with shish kebabs of nearly raw chicken liver and hot sauce.

Desi comes over to the table. He writes all the Warba material himself, but none of it is on record. "There's no financing," he says, "and no interest from the radio station or the newspaper." Local rhythms aren't commercial locally because the young people just don't care, he says; everyone likes to dance to Warba, but no one sees it as a pop commodity to be sought out on records. They think of pop stars as American, Cameroonian, and, especially, Zairian or Congolese. "In the 50s," Desi relates, "we didn't have any African popular music; it was all Caribbean or French, and then the Twist. And then in 1962, '63, or '64, the Zairians—Franco and Tabu Ley Rochereau—became very popular. All the dance bands started playing Zairian music." That included Desi's first band called Super-Volta, which he started in 1965, and which toured all over Upper Volta. James Brown became popular in Africa in the late 60s, and Desi added *le funky*, as he refers to soul music, to Super-Volta's repertoire. In the 70s he added reggae and a smattering of music from Cameroon and other francophone countries, but up to this day, the greatest demand is for the Congolese styles.

As if to demonstrate Desi's point, the band resumes playing. A single-picked guitar arpeggio leads to a military snare drum roll, and then to more guitar lines buzzing all over the place, and belted, tightly harmonized singing in Lingala—a Zairian language that seems mixed with French and has a lot of words that sound like "mama." The billows of guitar activity roll over a quick disco-like pulse from the bass drum. This is a currently popular song by Franco, and it no doubt will be played in thousands of clubs, bars, and discos all over West, Central, and East Africa that very same Saturday night. And the dancers are loving it. It's sensual, pelvic-rotation music, spiced generously with adages about love.

Local musicians might resent the dominance of Zairian or Congolese music, but local rhythms seem to get their chance sooner or later, as nationalism swells or promoters realize the sales potential of songs in a language that the local people can actually understand (which is not true of Lingala). A case in point is the growing popularity of Kenyan and Tanzanian groups in their own regions.

A similar lack of interest in local rhythms reigned in East Africa—Kenya and Tanzania—as recently as 1980, when the Voice of Kenya radio tried to replace international hits (Western and Congolese) with local music. The attempt fell flat, and the station marched the hit parade back on the air within two weeks. "Some young people buy Kenyan...music purely to have something to joke about," a local producer lamented to writers Roger Wallis and Kister Malm.

Kenya and Tanzania contain 140 cultural groups between them, each with its own language, and with Swahili and English as common languages. The market for popular music there dates from the 50s, when urban areas such as Nairobi and Dar-es-Salaam began to attract workers. Dance halls were established, their orchestras playing swing music and, in the early 60s, the Twist. (Rock's first impact in Africa seems to have come with Chubby Checker and the first rock 'n' roll dance. Africans have little use for foreign music without dances.) In the late 60s, Congolese music became available on imported 78s; then a wave of Zairian musicians arrived in person, many of them refugees from the Congolese War. By 1970, they completely dominated the music scene in both Kenya and Tanzania. But the 70s also saw the appearance of Kenyan groups singing in Luo, a Kenyan language, to their local *benga* beat. In Tanzania, big bands started to sing in Swahili. And in Africa, a change of language affects more than just the lyrics; Africa's languages are tonal, each with distinct intonations and rhythms that drastically change the music. The most popular East African groups, such as Orchestra Makassy, Super Mazembe, and Shika-Shika, continue to display a strong Zairian influence and to have Zairian members, but the Victoria Kings, Francis Fugwiti (the Kenyan Cowboy), and the Kilimambogo Brothers sing the local Luo, Kikuyu, and Wakamba languages to the benga beat. CBS, Island, and Virgin are beginning to record these groups in Nairobi studios, both for the local market and also to test their potential market in the rest of Africa and in Europe.

Until large-scale financing such as this comes to Upper Volta (which is a very poor country), Traore Desiree will have to compose his Warba music for the local dances only. He's actually bought an eight-track tape recorder, but there's no studio to put it in. In fact, if you peek into his pleasant garden and through his front door, you can see the machine sitting on top of a dresser. "The biggest problem, without a studio, is isolating the drums," Desi says.

Actually, the new government in Burkina Faso has been promoting local music of a sort, according to the vow in its national "Hymn to Culture": "It's a new Faso/That we will make known/Throughout the world . . . Beat the drums of our ancestors/Strike up the glorious march/The artists are ready/And they play/The hymn of victory." And they're not just talking about military brass bands, although there is one. In the past year, the government has bought instruments and amplifying equipment for about ten African rock-style ensembles, and has given equipment to groups of soldiers in various regions. They've also supplied equipment to an eleven-piece, all-girl band, les Colombes de la Revolution (The Doves of the Revolution), who practice in a cigarette-butt-strewn schoolroom and play at most official occasions in Ouagadougou. Their songs express themes similar to those of the "Hymn to Culture," arranged with local rhythms but more often in variations on reggae and Zairian music. These government-outfitted bands are the envy of the professional musicians, who are instrument-starved. "Les Colombes and the soldiers' bands are made up of people who had never played instruments before," a guitarist complains before a rehearsal at another Ougadougou club, the Don Camillo, as he carefully performs the daily task of getting all the red dust out of his equipment.

"We have to import all our instruments from France, and so they wind up being twice as expensive as in Europe. And when you translate that into Central African francs, it's impossible to get any materials."

But besides using music for propaganda purposes, the government and the military (actually one and the same) form bands because many of the leaders are musicians. Captain Thomas Sankara, the new thirty-five-year-old president of Burkina Faso, is known for his skill as a guitarist, and will frequently appear, unannounced, at some club around Ouagadougou. At every level, the government and development agencies in Ouagadougou are rife with musicians and ex-musicians. Until recently, Saidou Richard Traore, a native of the city who now works as a functionary with the American embassy there, composed, cut records, and led a large orchestra with sexy dancers that sold out the largest venues in the area. Ernest Nzekio, a Cameroonian working with the United Nations Development Program in close cooperation with Captain Sankara, was a guitarist who worked his way through college in the United States playing jazz.

But if he doesn't overthrow the government or go abroad to college and come back wearing a suit, ready to enter an agency, there's no way for a regional musician to make it big. He'll have to go to the big cities—join the masses streaming to the West Coast metropoli of Abidjan, Lagos, Kinshasa, Douala, and Dakar, in, respectively, the Ivory Coast, Nigeria, Zaire, Cameroon, and Senegal.

It is still hard for Westerners to imagine these sprawling conglomerations on a continent that evokes images of jungles, savanahs, deserts, the mountain gorilla, and the native village. Every day hundreds of people leave from the villages, driven away by drought, famine, or just the lack of anything to do. They're bound for the coastal cities on a train or bus, carrying a few belongings, a little savings, and the name of a distant relative. The lure, often illusory, is a better lifestyle. The rural and urban economies are actually based on completely different scales; a plantation worker in the Ivory Coast, which has the most stable economy in West Africa, might hope for 7,500 African francs a month (about fifteen dollars), while an urban textile worker could expect 35,000. The problem is that there aren't any textile jobs available in the city; there is very little industry at all and very few jobs compared to the enormous influx of people.

But unlike the situation in the villages, money does exist in the city, and everybody wants their chance to make it; so they keep coming, and the growth rate is astounding. From 137,000 inhabitants in 1950, Kinshasa jumped to two and one half million by 1976,

Jak Kilby

A street scene in Lagos, Nigeria.

three million by 1982, and is expected to double that figure by 1988. It now sprawls over about seventy square kilometers. Lagos, its population swelled by the oil boom of the 70s, is bulging even faster than Kinshasa, and its reputation as a center of crime and traffic strikes as much terror in the hearts of most Africans as the mention of New York City does to a Midwestern American. Abidjan, a metropolis with skyscrapers, shantytowns, and sections reminiscent of Paris, jumped from one hundred thousand in 1945 to over two million in 1985.

These cities were originally founded as ports for the colonial exploitation of resources, and their ability to employ and support a large population has not developed much beyond that. They have trickle-down economies in the truest sense. All the real money involves foreign business, and any business-suited Mercedes owner is usually involved in it. There are jobs providing services to these people, and those who fill these positions then have some money to purchase other goods and services, and so on down the line. But the top of the pyramid is much too narrow to support the bulk at the bottom, which includes the hundreds of thousands of recent arrivals. So, many young people wind up waiting around the shacks in the rambling suburban villages on the edge of the city, or in the inner city neighborhoods where dozens of ethnic groups live side by side, dreaming of "the good life" that's so close they could be run over by the Mercedes that symbolizes it.

Among these young dreamers are talented musicians from many ethnic groups, many others who can simply play guitar, and others who have yet to learn. In a crossroads like Abidjan, they may speak Senoufo, Baoule, Dioula, Mandingo, Bete, Malinke, Ga, or dozens of other languages. Fresh from their villages, they are imbued with their native rhythms, as well as with the Beatles songs that helped them learn to play rock instruments.

In the metropolis, these young people are bombarded by an even wider range of music. Pumping recorded music into the streets of Abidjan are the *maquis*, indoor/outdoor bars that specialize in huge beers and shish kebab. Each one has large speakers and a taped music collection. Often the owners come from diverse parts of Africa, and their taste is reflected in the music they play. So, in areas like Treichville or Washington, where the maquis are butted one against another, a walk down the street brings a smorgasbord of rhythm 'n' blues next to Congolese rhumba next to Afro-beat next to local music, such as Ziglibithy.

In the enclosed restaurants, the music may be more sedate, but the collections are even more eclectic. While the wife takes care of the customers and the food, the husband plays disc jockey, carefully selecting Louis Armstrong or Jim Reeves oldies and cleaning them before he puts them on the turntable.

Local radio schedules are full of every kind of music, from international Top Forty programs to features on regional cultures of the interior. International radio, including the Voice of America, Armed Forces Radio Network, the British Broadcasting Corporation, and Radio France International (RFI) are broadcast all over the continent. The RFI, emanating from the Avenue du President-Kennedy in Paris, offers the most balanced fare and gives a great deal of attention to modern African music, allowing the cross-fertilization of musical ideas within Africa and encouraging pan-African hits. One of the most complete and up-to-date archives of new African music in the world is maintained by the RFI, and every night the deejay Gilles—now a celebrity throughout Africa—hosts an African show called "Canal Tropical." The complete range of the RFI's music covers Africa with a powerful shortwave signal retransmitted from across the Atlantic in Guyana, South America.

The latest Euro-American dance hits, Zairian favorites, and local dance tunes are introduced in the discoteques in the cities. The range of disco atmospheres is vast and varied, from the mannered lounges of the intercontinental hotels to the plush hot spots in town and the multitude of small, tightly packed boxes in the night-crawling areas of the inner-city neighborhoods. There are the Phoenicia and the Paradise in Lagos, the Bustop in Accra, and the

Carleton Hotel in Monrovia, Liberia, to name just a few.

In Ouagadougou, the most popular club mixes mid-70s disco with the latest Congolese hits. The thirty-foot-square dance floor mercilessly and continuously explodes in the flash of strobe lights, and the walls feature black-light portraits of Stevie Wonder, Bob Marley, Michael Jackson, and the Rolling Stones (the last isn't exactly a portrait; it's a big tongue). Thick, brown velour couches line the periphery of the floor and waitresses come there to give meaningful handshakes and take requests for beer and Fanta. There's a one A.M. curfew in Ouagadougou, so the crowd disappears at midnight (soldiers shoot first and ask questions later on the street between one and five, it is said).

But in Abidjan, the frenzy lasts all night, with pelvis-to-pelvis dancing as the deejays growl "C'est Ça!" in the dozens of popular discos that line the streets of the Treichville neighborhood. In the higher-class places—such as the Safari, where employees wear *buana* hats and stuffed game hangs on the walls—the dancing is more self-conscious, with prostitutes in high-fashion clothing having the most relaxed time, while couples on dates dance seriously or sit on the couches watching lone dancers strut their stuff while they watch themselves appreciatively in the smoked mirrors.

Car radios, box radios, and record shop speakers all add their distorted sound to this musical potpourri. It may seem random but, like everywhere else, there are tastemakers at work. Local stations use any method to select their music, from contests to graft. But concerted promotional pushes are being carried out by the multinational record companies, for lately Africa has been recognized as a lucrative market.

Today, the big five multinational record companies—CBS, EMI, Polygram, WEA, and RCA—with their complex system of subsidiaries and licensing arrangements, wield a heavy, double-edged sword. They record local music and distribute it to local and, sometimes, international markets. Then they also promote and distribute Top Forties American and British hits with the same fervor that such music is promoted in the United States and Europe. The clout these multinationals have has been documented by musical economists Wallis and Malm: EMI, for example, "operates in every continent, through group companies in thirty-three overseas countries," boasts a company self-evaluation they have obtained. "Using hundreds of promotion men and over a thousand salesmen, it has the power to stimulate demand both in quantity and quality and to meet the demand when sales accelerate."

Earlier foreign music fads, such as rhumba and calypso, came through somewhat indirect routes that will be discussed later. Early rock fads, such as the Twist and Beatlemania, were only weakly promoted but spread like wildfire. Later rock and country-and-western music have both been pushed heavily by multinationals and local distributors at one time or another, and they continue to influence the composition of local music, but the market for country-and-western and rock has subsided in most countries. As Nigerian writer Joe "Hyena" Kadenge of *Africa Music* magazine warned foreign rock bands who want to tour Africa, "It is no longer enough to have a good beat and some clever guitars. Remember, you are playing to a tired, seen-it-all type of crowd." A crowd, it should be mentioned, that finds it hard to dance to a monolithic, heavy down-beat rhythm like the typical rock sound.

The first massive, coordinated push by the multinationals came with disco music in the mid-70s. This was, and continues to be, a worldwide effort that created a new term in the music business— mega-sellers, meaning recordings that sell over fifty million copies. In Africa, disco fit in well as an extension of the soul music that had become particularly attractive in the Africanized form developed by James Brown. And its black American artists, such as Rick James, Kool and the Gang, Shalamar, Stevie Wonder, and Lionel Ritchie,

A Ghanaian Michael Jackson impersonator about to be mobbed by African teenyboppers at a concert in London.

Jak Kilby

have continued to be popular after the 70s disco fad faded. It should not be surprising that the greatest promotional success of all times is Michael Jackson who, though not played much in discoteques, is the darling of most Africans under seventeen years of age. Jackson has also provided the latest youth fashion fad—his single, fingerless glove can be seen even on ragamuffins who sneak onto buses without paying—superseding the West African "Dallas" fashion fad. Breakdancing, or "the Smurf," has caught on in a highly gymnastic style performed to live funk or slow soul music, both in nightclub acts and nationally televised contests.

Modern jazz music is almost never heard except in South Africa, although almost every leading guitarist asked about jazz claims to have been influenced by George Benson. (Makossa star Manu Dibango, however, insists that members of village performance associations listen to jazz recordings to come up with new variations of local rhythms.)

The young immigrant to the city is much more limited in what he hears live than in what he hears on recordings and broadcasts. In the raucous Saturday night sessions of the open-air dance halls, he experiences the new urban dance music that he very well might play; in the streets he may be part of the urbanized celebration music, such as *gumbe*. African superstars on tour—such as the Zairians Franco and Rochereau—usually play in stadiums.

Live acts brought from outside Africa play in the sports stadiums as well. Lately, this has exclusively been funky music. Reggae groups who've toured recently have had a hard time, and it's been ten years since salsa tours have met with any success. Lesser-known black funk acts from the Antilles and the U.S. have an easier time of it: Dynasty, Delegation, Positive Force, Skyport, One-Way Al Hudson, Millie Jackson, to name a few. Sometimes these groups are brought to Africa with record company backing; more often, freelance promoters, in some way connected to a hot group, pop out of the woodwork when an opportunity arises. But the opportunities are often shady. For instance, in Abidjan recently, one promotion team fled the Hotel Ivoire, where they'd set up their office, after the bottom fell out of a tour of the Antillean group Kassav they'd tried to organize on borrowed money. They had booked the sports stadium and put up huge posters of the Kassav musicians all over town. They had convinced Georges Tai Benson, a prominent television personality, to give them free publicity on his program. As a result, the promoters sold all the tickets. The only problem was that they had never signed a contract with Kassav. And one day the bad news came—Kassav had been offered three times the money to do an exclusive tour for another group of promoters and would not be available for their concert. The failed promoters now run around town evading their creditors, once in a while sending a telex to Kassav entreating them to do one concert to recoup losses. Obviously, the music business below the multinational level in Africa is more than laissez-faire; it's virtually a free-for-all.

All levels of the music industry in Africa fall prey to this disorganization. Less-than-standard contracts mean musicians lose control of their royalties. Record companies, too, lose sight of their product and its income once they sell subsidiary record rights to another company, who, in turn, may sell subsidiary rights to five more regional companies. And even if the legitimate parties aren't trying to cheat one another, record piracy usually eats at least half the potential income of a popular recording.

In Nigeria, where the problem is particularly severe, record companies put stern warnings against illegal copying on their record jackets, promising "swift and brutal" legal action. But there's very little enforcement and the pirating operations run the gamut from the record store owner who will record your favorite songs onto a cassette, to the disc jockey who records new releases in the club onto a cassette which his family members then one by one reproduce in double-cassette box radios, to large companies in Singapore who re-master a record and sell shiploads of counterfeit records back to Africa. Cassette pirating is especially lucrative because very few people have record players or can afford records; a record may cost ten dollars—a small fortune in much of Africa—while the cassette costs two or three. Up-and-coming regional artists are the worst victims of piracy; their records first catch on with the local poor folk and the piracy losses completely wipe out even the small profits they might have made.

But the young musician with potential chooses to see none of this. What he focuses on, instead, is the big hoopla made over stars. In Abidjan, for example, a young immigrant is captivated by the brilliant television image of a short man in a gold lamé suit making his way across a wide stage with the loose-kneed, spasmodic shuffles of Ziglibithy—a traditional Bete rhythm—singing in disconcerting, full-throated Arabic tones to the accompaniment of the full orchestra of the Ivory Coast Television station. This is Bailly Spinto, a singer, composer, and dancer whose songs are often on top of the Ivory Coast charts. He had one that reached the second spot in all Africa, and once in a while he tours France.

As a boy in Abidjan, Spinto sang in school, in clubs, and in any neighborhood festival. In the early 70s, when he was eighteen, he finally formed a group called the New System Pop. His sound married the then-fashionable rhythm 'n' blues music of James

Brown, Otis Redding, and Wilson Pickett to local rhythms. Playing in nightclubs that attracted Europeans, he made international connections that enabled him to tour North Africa, Latin America, and Europe, returning to the Ivory Coast in 1975. He cut his first record, *Taxi Sougnon*, in 1979. It became an instant hit and established Spinto as an Ivory Coast institution. Since then, his hits have incorporated more of the rhythms of the region and the proverbs of traditional song, and less rhythm 'n' blues, which has secured respect for him from a loyal adult audience, but has taken him out of the world of instant youth hits.

Another local star—Alpha Blondy—whose hit "Cocody Rock" was playing in the Club Canari in Ouagadougou—is more of a role model for the young musician. Blondy gets mobbed by youths when he goes to the post office and turns 15,000-seat stadiums into scenes of delirium when he tours the Ivory Coast, Senegal, Togo, Benin, Mali, and the rest of West Africa.

Blondy, who has black hair, and whose real name is Seydou Kone, was born in 1953 in the provincial town of Dimbrokro, the Ivory Coast. He formed an Afro-rock group, the Atomic Vibrations, when he was in high school, but was sent to Liberia to complete his schooling and then to New York to study business at Columbia University. Working his way through school as a messenger, he began singing with Jamaican groups in New York, most notably with Monyaka. Producer Clive Hunt recorded six of Blondy's songs, but financial problems caused Blondy to return home before finishing the album.

Back home, Blondy's family was not at all happy with his musical ambitions. This is a common situation all over the world but especially in Africa, where professional musicians are traditionally low on the ladder of respect, and where—in modern times—a functionary with an MBA from a foreign university is a parent's dream. Blondy's parents went to unusual extremes to try to set him back on the right course, even having him kidnapped and put into a mental hospital. Shaken, he made no music for two years in the late 70s, supporting himself by doing English translations for the Ivory Coast television station.

At the station Blondy met the producer of a talent show called "First Chance," a regular broadcast in which one or two novice singers are interviewed by a television personality and then sing their own songs, backed by members of the television orchestra. The show is taken lightly by most viewers, to say the least. As one put it, "I'd rather see a show called 'Last Chance' where they'd pick up some old guy from the street and let him sing before they removed him from the city." The young singers, usually girls, give timid answers to trite questions, such as "Why did you start singing?" ("My friends liked my voice"), and "How do you like secretarial school?" ("I'm just going to please my mother"), while viewers giggle.

Blondy's debut on the show caused quite a stir and the ubiquitous producer, Georges Tai Benson, invited him to make a record, using the eight-track TV recording machine and the television musicians. The album, *Jah Glory,* all reggae as implied by its title, sold out its first pressing in one month and eventually became gold three times over, hitting charts all over Africa and in France. People everywhere sang along with the irresistible melody of "Brigadier Sabari" (which has an intro very similar to the beginning of "Attack of the Giant Ants" by the American Blondie).

Reggae, by the way, is not new in Africa, having been embraced in 1976 with the first international albums of Bob Marley and the Wailers. The fad has died down somewhat since 1979, but reggae and the rasta mystique remains a strong current in the urban youth culture. The term "rasta," however, is often used disparagingly in Africa and means a rebellious, Western-oriented youth. Blondy campaigns for a more respectable attitude in his song "Rasta Poue" ("Stoned Rasta"): "There are drunk rastas, crazy rastas, and *rastas cool.*" These last are the real, responsible rastas, he explains, and Alpha's take on reggae is as modernized African music. He reinjects it with lyrics in Dioula, Senoufo, and Baoule. This africanized reggae portrays to the world today's African, who, he says, "wears jeans and a t-shirt but has a very native way of speaking." This attitude, combined with a music that has a more celebratory lilt to it than its accusatory Jamaican cousin, makes Alpha and his music an irresistibly attractive role model for African youth.

Unfortunately, though, it's unlikely that the young would-be musician is going to follow in Blondy's footsteps. Most of today's successful African musicians either come from a middle-class family, or have been schooled for some profession. Many have even worked at an office job for a period of time. At the very least, they've had a scholarship to study abroad. Of course, there are exceptions to this rule. But it takes resources—money and personal connections—to get out of the rut that musicians who begin as members of the large dance bands find themselves in.

For example, a young man, newly arrived to the city, needing money and loving music, hears from a relative that there's an opening in the percussion section of the Mona Orchestra, led by Sax Zadi, the King of Zogbo. This is not an unusual occurrence, for the members of the Mona Orchestra are paid only a pittance, and thus are always ready to leave. So the young man presents himself at the

Many bands are connected to civic and military organizations. Les Amazones de Guinee are all policewomen.

Juliet Highet

Idriss Diabate

The bridge between the "African" section and the "European" section of Abidjan.

Club Mont Zatro in the suburb of Yopougon where Sax Zadi is currently playing, and is given a shaker (a gourd with a net of shells around it) that keeps a steady rhythmic pattern. He's told to keep an eye on the conga player; if this musician moves up to play the trap drums, the newer musician can take over congas. Eventually, in this way, he will learn guitar, keyboards, or horns, if he has the desire and talent. Meanwhile he's at least playing music and getting a dollar or two plus beer each night.

This young musician has just put himself into a very vulnerable position, and is probably on a dead-end trail. His skill is thought of as easily replaceable; he might never make enough money to buy his own instrument; he has no contract. He's at the complete mercy of the band operator, who may or may not be the bandleader, but, in any case, owns the instruments. Even if the band is as successful as possible, putting out albums and touring abroad, there is no guarantee that this young musician will make any money once the expenses (always heavy, considering the size of the band) are paid and the bandleader takes enough off the top to live like a star. For instance, there are still at least six members of a Sonny Okosun tour in the United States; they played dozens of sold-out concerts in one of the richest countries in the world, they made absolutely no money and they are too ashamed to go back to Nigeria.

Part of the problem lies with the dual attitude toward music-making in traditional African society. On the one hand, as Nigerian musicologist George Nwajei explains, "To the African, music is essentially a vehicle through which meaningful living is made possible, and without which life becomes monotonous." Music is a necessary part of any life-cycle event; an important part of the ambience of royal courts as well as the day-to-day activities of a village. On the other hand, much of this music is made by people who make their living as farmers or artisans; anyone who depends on music-making for their actual living is depending on the patronage of the few people who can pay for their services.

"If you ask people in my region about the status of a talking drummer," says Francis Awe, a drummer from Western Nigeria, "they will say they are beggars." Awe, who actually comes from a royal family, is using his position as a university lecturer in Lagos to try and elevate the status of musicians. For himself, it was "taboo for any member of the royal family to play the talking drum" because of the lowly status attached. (A talking drum is a drum that imitates speech patterns.) However, from the time he was two months old he claims he had an irresistible urge to play this instrument. "Whenever they played around our place, I always burst into unending crying, until my grandmother took me to the ... place they were playing, and then I stopped weeping.... I think I belong to those who are chosen by [fate] ... to be a talking drummer." Even so, Awe tried to keep away from drumming as a profession, stopping completely when it interfered with his studies. He

Floyd Webb

A young talking drummer in Lagos.

graduated and began working for the Ministry of Lands and Housing. But wherever he went, people somehow knew he was a talking drummer and would invite him to play. Finally, after being pursued by the university, he succumbed to his true profession. He realized that by teaching talking drumming he could perform a service for African musicians everywhere by giving their metier academic legitimacy. "I want for people to realize that whoever plays the talking drums is not a beggar. It is a profession, like a lawyer, like a doctor, like an engineer," he asserts. However, for the most part, Africans think of musicians as dropouts who couldn't apply themselves to a real profession.

Of course, earning steady money can in itself legitimize musicians. "If you go to, say, Oyo State," adds a student of Awe, "and you ask about talking drummers, they'll say, yes, they are beggars. But then they might add that there is this one guy who plays with Sunny Adé and drives an air-conditioned 504, and they'll say it with admiration." But this attitude is a sort of double bind, since most musicians will not be able to make a living with their craft until it is thought of as a craft that deserves decent pay. Until then, the band member, as Dr. Nwajei puts it, is "doomed to economic poverty," as well as parental disapproval and a generally unstable life. He may find girlfriends aplenty in the dance-hall environment. However, he must also be prepared to be left behind if she meets an engineer or an MBA who may also have just arrived in the city from the village, but has come by way of a European university and has a suit, a job, and a car. In fact, many of the original songs by dance-hall musicians are concerned with this subject.

Hopefully, the lot of the professional musician will change in Africa as the new popular music becomes more respected and fits into urban life the way traditional music fit into village life. As mentioned before, juju music is already accepted as appropriate for traditional and ceremonial Yoruba occasions. And much of the new music is gradually filling traditional roles: teaching, telling the news, commenting on changes in social mores, praising and criticizing public figures, and moving dancers around the floor in that urban celebration, Saturday Night. But, to completely fit into urban life, musicians must have their slot in the urban economy.

Meanwhile, as the crowd dances till dawn in the open-air dance hall of Yopougon, the young musician is playing an important role in the evolution of new music, reinjecting his regional rhythms and "roots" vitality into the urban mix. For it is here that the raw fusions are created and refined into the grand styles that are taken into the international limelight by the superstars of highlife, soukous, Afro-beat, juju, modern griot styles, mbaqanga, and makossa.

Billy Bergman

Church harmonies made their greatest impact along the coasts. This is the dedication ceremony of a new church in an Ivory Coast village, 1985.

D I S C O G R A P H Y

Olatunji	DRUMS OF PASSION	Columbia CL 1412
Various Artists	MUSIC FROM THE HEART OF AFRICA: BURUNDI	Nonesuch Explorers Series
Talking Heads	REMAIN IN LIGHT	Sire SRK 6095
Various Artists	MUSIC AND RHYTHM	PVC Records PVC 201
Various Artists	THE NAIROBI SOUND	Original OMA 101
Francis Bebey	AFRICAN SANZA	OZ 3312
Les Amazones de Guinee	AU COEUR DE PARIS	Cherry Red 76
Bailly Spinto	BEHI ZOKO	LIS Records 001
Alpha Blondy	COCODY ROCK	Pathe Marconi/EMI
Mick Fleetwood	THE VISITOR	RCA LP 5044

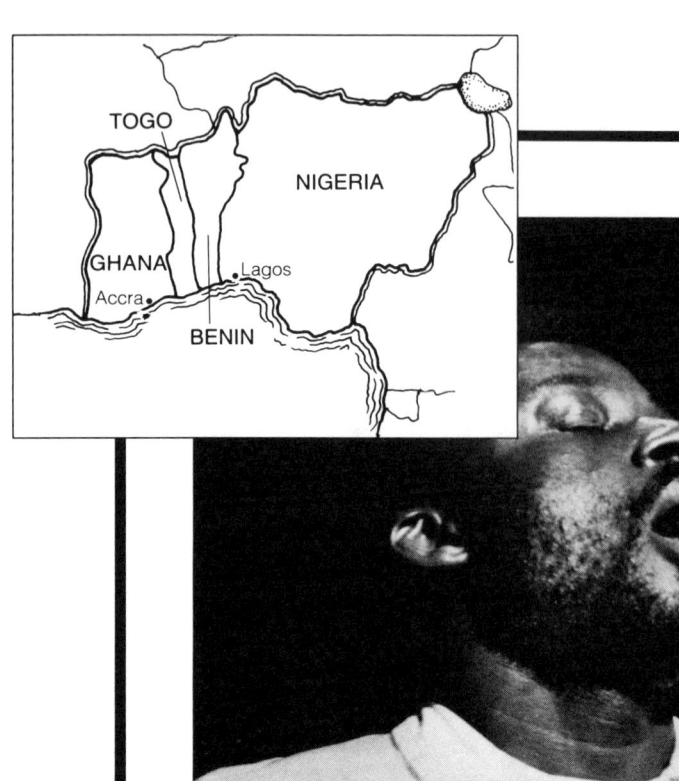

Jak Kilby

HIGHLIFE

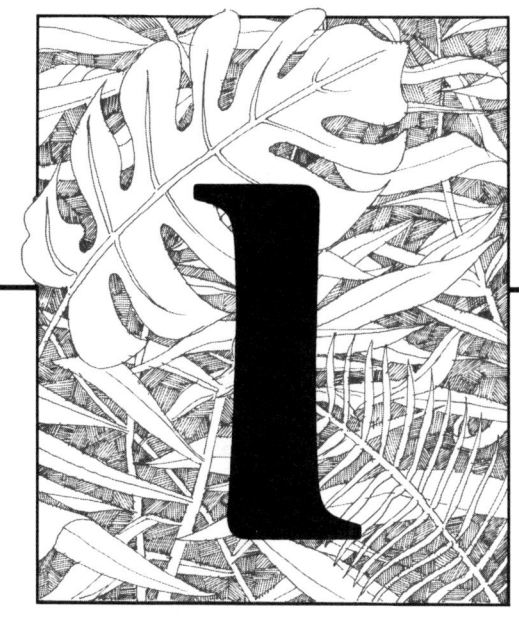

Chapter · Two

I t's all one, I tell you; it's all a unity!" These words, spoken by Paul Wassaba, one of the few professional arrangers who work with new African music, is the most comforting reply anyone could give to a question about the innumerable regional styles of traditional African music. The provocative variety of African rhythms and melodic styles is, of course, a mine that can provide infinite richness to future African sounds. There are a few characteristics, however, that are universal to the music throughout Africa south of the Sahara.

The most celebrated characteristic of all African music is its rhythmic nature. Of the three main elements in music—rhythm, harmony, and melody—the balance of interest in African sound lies in rhythm. In most Western music, the drama is created through harmony, as a piece moves away from its home chord or tonal center, and through a series of developments that may surprise the listener, wrench at his innards, or send him into sublime space before it finally finds its way back home. Meanwhile, the rhythm is just keeping time, like the regular beat of a metronome, making sure that all the parts of the harmonic mix come together at the correct moment. The opposite is true of African music. The harmony of a piece is the stable element. The rhythm creates the drama, unfolding in surprising and complicated ways.

One level of this drama that consistently occurs in African music is polyrhythm—two or more rhythms that run against each other. There are two basic types of rhythms: duple and triple. A duple measure means that there are two, four, or eight beats per measure, all multiples of two. Triple rhythms have three, six, or twelve beats per measure, all multiples of three. If both these rhythms started

George Darko, currently one of the most popular highlife performers.

out together on one, they would come back together at twelve, which is a multiple of both four (the number of beats in the most common duple measure) and three. The tension of polyrhythm creates the vibrant texture of the music.

But the cycles of repetition played by different instruments in African music don't always start and stop at the same time, and this adds other dimensions to the polyrhythmic drama. For instance, the starting points of different patterns can overlap, causing "cross-rhythms." They can overlap so the notes of one instrument fall between the notes of another, creating interlocking patterns. One whole piece might be organized around a long, complex pattern of repeating phrases before it repeats itself; this is usually played by a high-pitched instrument such as a bell, a stick and a bottle, or hand-clapping. Any one instrument might repeat a shorter modular phrase or a series of phrases that are added together in various ways before they repeat. On top of this, or actually on the bottom, the lowest-pitched drums usually have the most freedom—the master drummer's improvisations.

Obviously, with this kind of rhythmic complexity, musicians are not counting measures. What keeps everyone playing at the same rate is a quick pulse that never changes and, for that matter, is never played, for it is much faster than the main beat that is heard. It is kept in the players'—and the dancers'—heads.

Since the same elementary pulse is in the dancer's mind, dancers are not tied to the emphasized beats of the instruments. They add, instead, the final layer of rhythm—the visual one—to the music. So most traditional African music is not complete without dancing. "In the performance of the full dance with singing and drumming," says musicologist A.M. Jones, "we have the flower of African musical genius, the highest manifestation of his art, and the most spontaneously creative expression of the soul within him." Except for some of the griot styles, all the new African music is also incomplete without dancing; it has developed and still finds full expression in the urban dance halls.

There were many types of harmony in the music of Africa before the Europeans came, but this is the one aspect of the music that was changed the most by them. "In traditional African music these days," says musicologist Andrew Tracey, "you almost never hear the original harmony. There's always someone putting in that third note and you have this sickly-sounding Western harmony all the time." The third note that Tracey refers to is the middle note in the stacked triads that form a chord. That middle note is often left out in traditional African music, creating what's called "open harmony." "The open harmony," Tracey continues, "had a different sound and

Jak Kilby

Some claim that Adakam music, like that played by this group from Akrobi, Northern Ghana, is a forerunner of both highlife and juju.

allowed for more freedom of movement. It used to be that you'd have the words first, and then get an idea of the melody from that. Now you have this chord structure and you're linked to a fixed stereotyped circle."

Obviously Tracey doesn't approve of this change. But lush harmony was the most attractive characteristic of Western music to Africans when they were introduced to four-part church singing by the missionaries, and the influence of Western music on the new popular music is most evident there. If Africans were going to use European harmony, they wanted to take advantage of its diatonic harmonies—full major and minor chords—arranged in the most effective progression, from the one to the four to the five chord and back to the one, the complete classical cadence. They weren't interested, according to Jones, in the complex shifting of chords that can exist in church organums or fugues. "They want above all," says Jones, "to savor, relish, and linger, upon the gorgeous sound made by a diatonic triad: the simpler the progression, the better they appreciate it." There's complexity enough in the rhythms of which these Western harmonies are an added element.

The missionaries introduced church melodies to the Africans as well, but melody had less influence on African music. Melody in Africa is to a large extent determined by the intonation of the languages. When the missionaries got Africans to sing the Doctrine in their own languages to simple church tunes, they thought they were scoring one for God. What they didn't always know, though, was that the Africans were not always singing what the missionaries thought they were singing. In the tonal languages, the meaning changes with the intonation, so if the same words are set into strict church tunes, the intonation changes so the meanings are different. Tracey found a version of the hymn "Angels from the Realms of Glory" translated into Ibo (Eastern Nigeria) as "There is no sorrow in heaven." When the same Ibo phrase was put into three different church tunes, however, it meant, respectively, "There are no tears on the bicycle," "There is no clothing among the crowd," and "There are no eggs in the sky" because of the changes in intonation.

Other early Western musical influences came via the military. Regimental bands existed in West Coast colonies as far back as the 1600s, but the first ones that seemed to make a major impact on local music were the ones in British outposts on the Gold Coast, present-day Ghana. The bands that had the most influence were often made up of troops from the British West Indies—Jamaicans, Trinidadians, etc. In the 1870s, for example, there is some evidence of members of the West Indian Rifles Band teaching brass band music to Ghanaians.

Thus a process of musical change began that John Collins, a chronicler, musician, and producer of new West African music, describes as having three main aspects. The first is the direct copying of Western music by Africans and a tendency for the resulting music to be re-Africanized as it becomes more popular and spreads inland. The second is the dynamics between Afro-American forms of music and African music itself. Caribbean, Latin-American, and, later, swing and soul music became models for the developing pop forms because they contained—in their African roots—possibilities for complex rhythms, yet repeated in patterns conducive to chord changes with dance-band instruments. And the Latin-American *clave* beat, the backbone of much Afro-American music, gives a polyrhythmic, three against two, feeling within a standard, four-beat measure. The third main aspect of the process is nationalism and local pride, which became a major force in the re-Africanization of the music after nations began gaining their independence around 1960 and musicians were encouraged to re-Africanize the music. These three factors, Collins maintains, add up to a reversal of previous assumptions, that the popular music of

Africa is becoming more Westernized; it's actually, on the whole, the other way around. Regional styles are evidence of this, and an early and clear example is highlife.

The Ghanaian brass band members would, for example, introduce local tunes arranged for marching bands into their repertoire. Then, when they played marching band music again it would be more syncopated. Military-trained African band members would take jobs playing in dance halls in Cape Coast for the new African elite that was developing there during the 1920s. These Westernized, urban, materially endowed Africans celebrated their status by copying Western ways of enjoying themselves—the musicians had to play waltzes and quicksteps. At first they exactly copied the European versions of these dances, then gradually developed their own, more syncopated style, called *abaha* music. Musicologist David Copeland suggests that it was the poorer urban folk, crowding around the outside of the dance halls, peering at the resplendent scenes through the ventilation openings, who first coined the name "highlife" for the scene. Probably motivated by equal parts of derision, admiration, and envy, the term was eventually picked up by the musicians of the dance bands to refer to their music.

Meanwhile, the people outside the dance halls looking in began adapting the music to their own needs. They replaced the brass with local instruments because the brass were much too expensive. They kept the drums and the military march feeling and added more vocal parts. This version of brass band music spread inland, where a dance form called konkomba was developed. Konkomba featured contests between dance groups lined up army-style and dressed in fancy costumes of shorts, peaked caps, and colorful handkerchiefs.

At the same time, a form of highlife featuring guitar instead of brass was developing, thought to have been first introduced by Kru (Liberian) sailors who steamed along the coast as far south as Zaire and as far afield as the Caribbean. Since they hung out in bars that served palm wine, the music became known as "palm wine" music. Local melodies, mainly of the Akan language in Ghana, were adapted to this guitar style. The result is referred to as the "mainline" highlife feel, with prototypes such as the song "Yaa Amponsah" establishing the characteristics of offbeat bass lines and picking in the traditional style used for Akan stringed instruments such as the seprewa. Other sailor's instruments, such as the accordion and the concertina, were incorporated. The palm wine music began to mingle with non-ceremonial music such as game songs, and the new forms of celebration music spreading from city to city, such as the *gumbe* for percussion and harmonized voices. In the bush, minor scales were used in some of the guitar highlife, drawing it closer to local pentatonic scales; this is called blues though it sounds nothing like American blues.

During World War II, thousands of British and American troops were stationed in Ghana, and the musicians among them formed swing bands with local musicians. One very famous band, formed by a Scottish sergeant, was called Sergeant Pepper and His Black and White Spots. Another, a jazz quartet called the Tempos, was formed by members of the Spots and became popular as well. A sideman of the Tempos, E.T. Mensah, took over when the other leaders went back to Britain at the end of the war. Mensah's new band combined brass band music with swing and with other emerging forms of highlife, such as "concert party" (actually a show imitating minstrels from the U.S.—the black performers wore white lines around their lips in an attempt to look like whites in blackface). Palm wine music and calypso, which was a West African fad at the time, both became part of the new mix. Around 1950, E.K. Nyama formed E.K.'s Band, adding more Afro-Cuban elements to highlife, replacing the local drums with congas and bongos and beefing up the horn riffs.

The 50s and early 60s were high times for highlife, then in its mature form. Highlife bands were booked for society gigs, upper-class nightclubs, recordings, and tours. E.T. Mensah became known as the King of Highlife—assuming the first throne of the new

Hi-Life International upholds the highlife tradition with wide-ranging fusions in London.

Jak Kilby

pop music—and put out dozens of top-selling records for Decca Records. His and other bands toured extensively through Africa, returning most often to Nigeria, Liberia, and Sierra Leone, countries of similar musical influences. In turn, highlife bands began forming in these countries.

The force of nationalism came behind highlife in 1957, when Ghana achieved independence. In many African countries, musicians will date the beginning of the growth of their own popular music style from the date they gained independence from their colonial ruler. Control of radio stations is one important factor. But Ghana, with its relatively early freedom date, gained an extra asset: Kwame Nkrumah, its first president. Nkrumah, returning to Ghana in 1947 after twelve years of education in the United States and the United Kingdom, had developed a coherent philosophy for the development of a free Africa. The tenets of this philosophy included the political unification of black Africa and the encouragement of modern expression of indigenous culture. Nkrumah embraced highlife music as a bona fide modern African music and created institutions and fellowships for the advancement of its musicians, both in Ghana and abroad. Around 1960, he tried to change the name highlife to something more African-sounding, such as *osibisiba,* but this change was rejected by musicians, since the music was already known far and wide.

The music itself continued to straddle various foreign categories, picking up touches from new fads as they came along and from the traditional rhythms that were fresh in the minds of the musicians. Some groups, such as the West African Brothers Band, were made up entirely of traditional musicians who had been trained to play modern instruments. "What happened was that in those days," E.T. Mensah told journalist Ndubuisi Okwechime, "we urgently wanted an indigenous type of rhythm to replace the fast-fading foreign music of waltz, rhumba, etc. We evolved a music type there after relying on basic African rhythms. A crisscross cultural sound, so to speak. Therefore, no one really can lay claim to its creation, it had always been there, entrenched in West African culture. What I did was to give highlife world acceptance."

Today highlife sounds like the common denominator between African and Caribbean music. It is hard to say which parts of the music came from which parts of the world, since both came from very similar influences and the ideas steamed back and forth with sailors and soldiers. For example, when Louis Armstrong came to Accra in 1956, he was greeted by E.T. Mensah's band playing the highlife song, "All for You, E.T." Armstrong said that he knew the tune as a Creole song from his childhood in Louisiana.

In the late 50s and the 60s, Nigerians took the lead in the further development of highlife, as local music had not yet been adapted for local dance bands, who were playing swing and other Western pop. So Nigerian highlife stars began to arise, such as Rex Jim Lawson, and Dr. Victor Olaiya, known as "The Evil Genius of Highlife." Nigerian music picked up foreign cues from the new youth pop culture, and its African cues came from the awakening interest in regional rhythms.

Bridging all these elements is the venerable Sir Victor Uwaifo, who now produces a weekly television show from his own studios in Onitsha, Nigeria. Uwaifo was the twelfth in a family of thirteen children, the son of a police sergeant in Edo, Benin. As a youth, he discovered his talent for playing stringed instruments but, as was expected of him, he finished his education at the Yaba Technical School, and became a graphic artist for the Nigerian Television Service. However, as early as 1959, while he was still in secondary school, he played with Victor Olaiya and His All Stars, and then with Isi Orisi and His Music. In those days, says Uwaifo, "You couldn't have been any musician to be reckoned with unless you played waltzes, quicksteps, boleros, cha cha cha, and mostly Nat King Cole songs in the nightclubs, as well as highlife music." Uwaifo's technical abilities on the guitar (he could do scales and modal improvisations besides just imitating chorded riffs) pushed him quickly to the front of the band. Soon, he introduced lead guitar lines, his first innovation. Formerly, he says, "the guitar was used like a rhythm instrument. There was nothing like lead." In 1964, he played on a Lagos television show, "The Minstrels," with a guitar, conga, and bass trio. Television being what it is, the trio became quite popular and were known as "The Trio."

But Uwaifo wanted to keep working with highlife, so he gathered musicians and formed the ten-piece Melody Maestros dance group in 1965. He knew his band would have a hard time fitting into the market because they were not from a major ethnic group—Ibo or Yoruba—so he had to come up with something new. He replaced the stand-up bass then being used by highlife bands with an electric bass after hearing Franco use it in 1963 and being impressed by its big sound. Electricity also allowed the bass line to move around more easily, and to become an active voice in itself. Uwaifo also added the local Akwete rhythm to the mix, along with a little Chubby Checker: "They were twisting to everything then." The result was his first hit, "Joromi," that "catapulted me into the limelight," he remembers. He became so popular in Nigeria and Ghana that, unknown to him, the name of one of his later hits, "Guitar Boy," was used as the code name for an attempted coup in

Ghana. Operation Guitar Boy failed and, for a while, Uwaifo's music was banned in Ghana.

Still Uwaifo's popularity grew as he infused his music with more and more rock 'n' roll energy. This is more unusual than the connection between African music and dancing would imply. As John Miller Chernoff points out, Africa is more attracted to the "aesthetic of cool" than to the frenzied hijinks of American and British performers. But, says Uwaifo, "I was an athlete, right from the word go...and I've seen people like Elvis Presley play and sing and dance....Why should I sit down? And there was this Cliff Richard also and the Shadows and I said, boy...if I am to play music at all, I have to really move and jump." He introduced dances coordinated with each of his new rhythms, such as the Shadow Dance, which he thought up when he tried to pick up his shadow. It consists of moves like "The Umbrella," where one hand is lowered and the other raised like it's holding an umbrella. The whole audience would do it. "I would yell 'Shadow, Shadow!' and they would reply, 'Uh, huhhh.' " He found it wasn't difficult to get audience participation, something that's traditional to African performance. "It's spontaneous; they respond without even asking them."

Throughout the early 70s, Uwaifo continued to develop African highlife dances that corresponded to international pop trends. For instance, Mutaba had the soul feeling at that time, and Uwaifo would rap in different languages over the music. When reggae came around, Uwaifo was already playing something he called *akassa*, which, coincidently, sounded very much like the Jamaican rage. So to pick up reggae, he merely added "rapping, talking about all these things, freedom." After akassa, Uwaifo went on to *titibiti*, which means eagle, a style he let loose to fly where it wanted, incorporating any type of music he felt like. By 1973, he had gold discs, knighthood (albeit conferred by a local college), and an invitation to play at the Roundhouse in London. The British were shocked when they came to hear African music and saw Uwaifo "grinding at the organ and jumping around." He spent the rest of his stay in Britain explaining to critics that "changing from a quill to a Parker pen wouldn't change the words that a historian was writing. And they agreed with me in the end."

Highlife's wide spread of influences led it to combine, early on, with other popular styles that were developing in Africa. A typical case is the highlife of Prince Nico Mbarga, whose father was Cameroonian, but who grew up in Cross River State, Nigeria, among the Ejara-speaking Etung people. "As I am born from this side and that side, I try to put these two things together...a sort of mixture of Nigerian and Cameroonian music." He calls his music *panco* highlife, a tribute to a dance rhythm he learned as a child.

Prince Nico actually started playing music in 1969, in Cameroon, where his family had fled to escape the horrors of the Nigerian Civil War (also known as the Biafran War). There he joined a hotel band called the Melody Orchestra, which played both highlife and Congolese music. Starting with conga drums, he worked his way up through trap drums and bass guitar to rhythm guitar and, eventually, lead guitar. He returned to Nigeria in 1972, along with some of the other Cameroonian band members, and started an orchestra at the Plaza Hotel, with the bandleader from Melody Orchestra. The hotel proprietor encouraged and financed the band to record, so Nico began writing his own songs. When the bandleader left the orchestra, Nico assumed the position. "I am from this side and from that side and I am the smallest," he said. "I must be the bandleader." He renamed the band "Rockafil Jazz," which many people assume is also the kind of music he plays. Then they criticize him because he isn't playing jazz. But according to Nico, the name doesn't refer to the music. It's an acronym for all the founding members of the group: R for Richard, O for Oji, C for Clement, K for Koli, etc. Rockafil's first song on the Phillips label, "I No Go Marry Me Papa," was a big hit in 1973. But the 45s he issued in the following years were busts, except for one small hit, the profits from which were used to bring presents home to the people in his mother's village in Cross River State.

Africans in general seem to have a very strong attachment to their mothers. For instance, when they ignore their mothers for long periods of time, they seem to be prone to hysterical fits of guilt, saying, "You don't understand, she's my mother! My only mother!" Nico's visit to his mother's house evoked these strong sentiments, and he wrote "Sweet Mother," singing, "If you forget your mother/ You lost your life." The album *Sweet Mother* became a huge hit across Africa in 1976; according to Nico, it is the largest-selling African album yet. Not only does it touch on a strong emotional issue; it is also the height of Prince Nico's panco style, which has the irresistibly happy chording of the best highlife along with the frenetic guitar activity of Congolese music and the jumping broken drum rolls of the Congolese/Kenyan benga style without any horns.

Prince Nico has never equaled the success of "Sweet Mother," but continues to produce records, now under his own label, and has toured in Europe. He also operates a nightclub in Onitsha and has built a larger one in Calabar, Cross River State, where his mother lives—the "Sweet Mother Hotel." He hopes to retire there.

Where does his royal title come from? "I'm a self-made prince," he says. "In Nigeria, if you are a chief of a village, you say you are a

Prince Nico Mbarga of "Sweet Mother" fame performs in London.

Jak Kilby

king . . . all of this, we are just doing it." His heredity is not of royalty. "I wanted to add something to my name to make it sweet. Some people cannot even pronounce the Mbarga. So, Prince Nico."

Nico's pidgin lyrics are in the tradition of pidgin highlife, which has a lot in common with Caribbean calypso. In that tradition, Nico comments and philosophizes on social mores, sprinkling little pre-scriptions through his songs. The language also allows him to communicate much more widely than just with his own small ethnic group. He has written songs in Yoruba, though. "When I want to compose with Yoruba language, I keep a Yoruba person and write in English whatever I want, and he will translate, all with the intonation . . . and when you hear it you will not believe I am not a Yoruba man," even though Nico speaks no Yoruba at all.

The transnational nature of Rockafil Jazz has recently caused Prince Nico some problems, however, when the Nigerian govern-ment started ordering foreign nationals out of the country. Up until 1982, Rockafil Jazz had nine Cameroonian members, most of whom had no passports. Prince Nico was allowed to keep only five Cameroonians in the country, two of whom left out of loyalty to the banished members. So in 1983, he had to rebuild his band with Nigerians, which has taken a toll on his music.

Jak Kilby

Koo Nimo (right) preserves the early—guitar and percussion—form of highlife.

Highlife in general has been having problems lately. Its association with fox-trot hotel bands makes it seem old-fashioned. Indeed, it retains many characteristics of its older pioneering days and the pop fads then. It has a slower, sweeter guitar chording more suited to acoustic instruments than to the new electric sounds, and a cadence more suitable to Latin American rhythms than to the newer, up-front regional drumming.

But, because it has been a ground-breaking music, there remains a constant interest in keeping it around. Koo Nimo, for example—who, as Daniel Amponsah, is chief technician in the Biochemistry Department at the University of Kumasi, Ghana—has been very busy in recent years playing older acoustic-guitar highlife around the world. "I'm always honored by representing my country," he told photographer Jak Kilby. "I'm proud to wear my kente or adinkra cloth as I'm playing a role in the community of nations as one of Ghana's cultural ambassadors. You see, I'm educating the younger people to respect traditional wisdom." In the same educational and nostalgic spirit, E.T. Mensah and Victor Olaiya have recently put out compilation albums of their classics. And, to some extent, highlife has been embraced by Ghanaians as their national music—to be fused, developed, and modernized however they see fit. The group Kantata (now based in Berlin) echoed this sentiment in their reply to a question about why they play highlife: "Because we are from Ghana and highlife is the music of our country." They have preserved the sound so today the younger crop of highlife musicians can play freely with the form: Mohammed Malcom Ben and His African Feeling Organization, Hi-Life International, and the African Brothers Dance Band International of Ghana.

Regardless of whether highlife remains a marketable music in its own right, Olaiya and Mensah feel satisfied because it has served an important function: "to allow for the development of other African musical forms," as Olaiya puts it. "All forms that emerged are in fact distant offshoots of highlife so, in fact, highlife music did not loose its hold, it only transformed itself into more dynamic tunes."

D I S C O G R A P H Y

Traditional Artists	UNESCO COLLECTION: AN ANTHOLOGY OF AFRICAN MUSIC	Barenreiter-Musicaphon
Traditional Artists	AFRICA SOUTH OF THE SAHARA	Folkways FE 4503
Traditional Artists	EWE MUSIC OF GHANA	Asch AHM 4222
Various Artists	AFRICA DANCES	Authentic Music 601
Various Artists	THE GUITAR AND THE GUN	Cherry Red ADRY 1
Victor Uwaifo	BEST OF VICTOR UWAIFO: Volume I	Polygram 046
Dr. Victor Olaiya	HIGHLIFE REINCARNATION	Polygram 073
Prince Nico Mbarga	SWEET MOTHER	Rounder 5007
George Darko	HIGHLIFE TIME	Celluloid 6726
Mohammed Malcolm Ben	AFRICAN FEELING	Sterns 1001
Hi-Life International	NA WA FOR YOU	Sterns 1006
Orchestra Jazira	LOVE DANCE MIX	Blackmarket 12-001

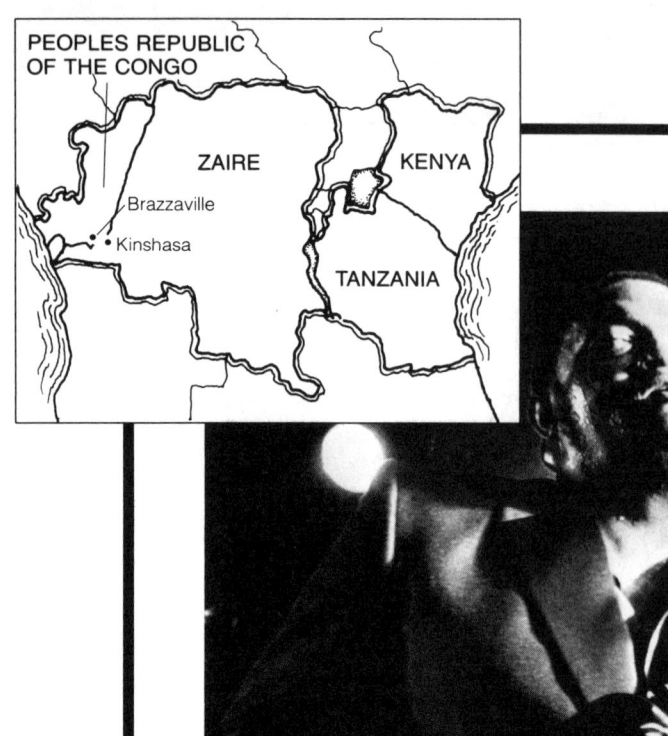

PEOPLES REPUBLIC
OF THE CONGO

ZAIRE

KENYA

Brazzaville

Kinshasa

TANZANIA

Jak Kilby

SOUKOUS

Chapter · Three

In an immense national sports stadium in a black African nation, banners proclaiming the slogans of a new government sway in the evening *harmattan* breeze. Another reads "The People Welcome Rochereau." Meanwhile, thousands of people from the city and surrounding villages make their way to the ticket buildings separated from the stadium by a wide parking lot, empty except for a few military vehicles.

The concert of Zairians Tabu Ley Rochereau and M'bilia Bel was scheduled to begin at four P.M., but at five-thirty the audience is just beginning to file in. The cheapest sections of the stands fill up first, behind and to the sides of the stage. By six o'clock, most of the musicians have made their way across the wide soccer field to the center platform. They begin playing a slow rhythm 'n' blues jam, move into a quicker funk pace, then stop. The music starts again, this time weaving the complicated guitar lines of Congolese music as Rochereau himself emerges onto the field in a white suit jacket. The crowd roars. The Seigner, as he is called, sings in French and Lingala about problems of love, and the spectators in the cheap seats jump to their feet and start dancing in place. Soon the Rocherettes, four sumptuous young women in leotards with cloths teasingly slung around their hips, rush out and begin to move sensuously in a dance choreographed by Rochereau and based on Congolese traditional steps. The crowd is excited, hooting and hollering as each dancer tries to outdo the others, sinking down, bouncing, collapsing, and thrusting.

Singer M'bilia Bel, Rochereau's protege, does not appear; she stayed in Paris because she is much closer to giving birth than she had previously thought. An up-and-coming Zairian chanteuse is

Franco, the Sorcerer of the Guitar, casts his dancing spell.

given a chance to fill in. Then Rochereau brings the crowd to new heights by touring the circumference of the stadium with the Rocherettes. The dancers bounce for each section, winding up with an invitation to local boys to come to the stage and compete to keep dancing there with the women.

This scene could have taken place in Senegal, Kenya, Burkina Faso, Tanzania, Gambia, Nigeria, Centeral Africa, or, of course, in Zaire or Congo-Brazzaville. It could be today or 1965 or anytime in between. Congolese music has ruled the pop scene in most of black Africa for over twenty years. It's appropriate to catch it in a sports stadium: the pan-African passion for Congolese music is almost as universal as that for soccer.

Congolese popular music, or *soukous*—"having a good time" music—its punchy modern form, is a mainstay of African entertainment for many reasons. It's irresistibly happy music; the busy-bee guitars, jaunting bass, and punchy brass have a cheery interplay whether the music is joking about the daily habits of city dwellers or mourning the passing of a great musician. It's unabashed dance music, without the terse philosophizing of highlife. Its layers of instruments allow complex rhythms as well as a quick, disco-esque pulse that mixes well with disco music when the two are alternated at popular deejay dancing bars.

Congolese music caught on quickly in the 60s in part because of long-term political unrest in Zaire. Zaire is the former Belgian Congo; the present Republic of the Congo, or Congo-Brazzaville, was the French Congo. The musical life of both countries is unified by the fact that their two major urban centers—Kinshasa (formerly Leopoldville) in Zaire and Brazzaville in the Congo—face each other across the Congo/Zaire river. Records are much cheaper in Brazzaville than in Kinshasa, so there's a lot of smuggling back and forth. The larger city, Kinshasa, has produced more international stars, though right now Brazzaville has the only serviceable recording studio in the two cities.

It wasn't long after Zaire gained its independence in 1960 that problems started. The province of Katanga and part of Kasai tried to secede from the country, and United Nations troops were called in. Patrice Lumumba, the first premier, was assassinated in 1961. For the next few years, leadership in the government was uncertain and secessionist revolts continued. Finally, in 1965, General Joseph Mobutu took over in a coup and hired mercenaries to bring all the provinces under the control of the central government. Meanwhile, musicians had taken refuge in neighboring countries such as Kenya, Uganda, and Tanzania. Many of them recognized that there was a great demand for their music in these countries and less competition than in Zaire. They could make a good living, so they stayed. A stream of hits on 78s and from live tours by both Rochereau and, most importantly, Franco, has kept Congolese music hot up to the present day.

Franco was born Francis L'Okanga La Ndju Pene Luambo Makiadi in 1938 in a village called Sona-Bata, about forty-five miles from Kinshasa. The last name Makiadi, which roughly means "susceptible to misfortune" in the local Kikongo Bantu language, was given to him because when he was a child "he had the troublesome habit of dying regularly," as his mother is quoted in a 1983 concert program. Her careful nurturing and the local nun's healthcare center kept him alive until he finally blossomed at the age of seven and began playing soccer with a vengeance. Too young to play in the more important interdistrict games, he encouraged his team by playing local Kebo melodies on a guitar he had made from a tin can and nylon string.

When Franco was ten, his father's death left the family in poverty and forced his mother to sell fritters in the market. Franco dropped out of school and devoted himself to soccer, but he would often sit with his mother in the marketplace, playing the tin-can guitar to attract customers. His music also attracted bandleader Ebengo Dewayon, who invited Franco, then twelve years old, to join his newly formed group, Watam, which consisted of two guitars and small patenge drums.

Guitarists and guitar groups like Watam were springing up all over Zaire at that time. They developed a guitar style similar to Bantu hand-piano playing, including quick runs on single-picked strings. Musicologist Hugh Tracey heard one guitarist, Mwenda Jean Bosco, playing and singing in the streets of Jadotville, Katanga province in 1949. Tracey was bowled over by the music and recorded several of Bosco's songs. One in particular, "Masanga," which tells of Bosco's departure from his village to come to Jadotville, gained international acclaim when released by Gallotone and later, Decca. The "Masanga" recording won prizes, and the tune was woven into Sir William Walton's "Johannesburg Festival Overture." Mwenda Jean Bosco, however, disappeared.

Guitar groups at the time were also playing various kinds of Cuban music. Proto-highlife bands from the coast (called "Coast Boys"), as well as transplanted Caribbean bands first brought in rhumba, pachanga, and cha cha cha. The music caught on in the cities, where bands would produce exact copies of the Latin numbers, even singing the lyrics in Spanish. Throughout the 60s and 70s, New York salsa producers found a ready and enthusiastic market for their records in Zaire, and a large salsa festival was organized to accompany the Ali–Foreman fight that was held there.

In the 50s, with Franco's help, the Watam guitar group became famous throughout the country. In 1953, they were asked to record with Loningisa Records, newly founded by a Greek businessman in Kinshasa. The businessman, Papadimitriou, was amazed by Franco's sinuous guitar playing and gave him the guitar he used during the recording sessions. Franco now owned his first real instrument, and later that year he composed and recorded "Bolingo na ngai na Beatrice" ("My love for Beatrice"), which became Loningisa's first big hit. Papadimitriou signed Franco into a ten-year contract, and during the next few years, Franco's records topped the hit parades four times. The owners of dance halls constantly requested that he play on party nights, but Franco had no instruments for a band since he used Loningisa's equipment for recording. So, every Saturday night for a year, Franco and his musicians would wait until dark, then secretly load the studio equipment into the studio's truck so they could play a "dancing." But Papadimitriou got wind of the trick one day and took back his instruments in a fury. However, the owner of the Chez Cassien dance hall came up with guitars, built traditional drums, and bought flutes for that Cuban flavor. With these instruments, on June 6, 1956, Franco christened his first band, O.K. Jazz.

Throughout the 50s, the Congolese bands started replacing Spanish lyrics with Lingala or Zairian patois, beginning the Africanization process. The earlier African lyrics, as John Storm Roberts points out, either dictated the melody line, which might have helped the music break away from Cuban melody, or fought it, which was awkward. Later, a handy truce was developed, in which one of the two vocal lines would ride the speech-tone patterns while the other would harmonize in thirds along a freer line. In this way, smoother melodies could be created without the loss of the meaning or the musical interest of the language itself.

What really Africanized the Congolese rhumba—and started its evolution into the modern soukous—was the introduction of electric guitars around 1958. Now, the twinkling patterns of lutes and hand pianos as transposed to guitar could shower fugues over the drums and horns; an electric bass could jump around to create the big sound that Victor Uwaifo wanted for his highlife. There are usually three guitars, as well as the bass, in electric Congolese bands. The guitars—solo, half-solo, and accompanying—cross and play with each other in short phrases, runs, and rhythms. By 1960, when Zaire gained its independence, Africa was awash with the amplified music emanating from Radio Leopoldville. The whole continent celebrated a new era with Grand Kalle, the reigning king of Congo-

The first guitar of many African musicians is made from an oilcan.

lese rhumba, and his hit "Independence Cha cha."

Soon after, Franco made a triumphant reentry into Kinshasa with the success of his song "Musumbuku." O.K. Jazz grew from its original nine members to a thirty-seven-man troupe known as T.P.O.K. Jazz, meaning *tout puissant,* or "all powerful" O.K. Jazz. (Jazz, of course, as in Nico's Rockafil, doesn't mean bebop, but instead denotes a pop group.) Franco himself, now a healthy 270 pounds, became known as the Grand Sorcerer of the Guitar. As Maître Taureau, a prominent show producer of the 60s, said, "The sounds of his guitar penetrate us and make us dance even when we don't want to." And through all the new dances introduced by various groups—the boucher, kiri-kiri, kaivasha, soukouma, and finally soukous—with the increasing bang of rock 'n' roll in the music, Franco, along with Rochereau, Prince Nico, and Papa Wemba kept the listeners dancing.

Now, more than thirty-five years since the start of his musical career, Franco has toured the Congo, Chad, Togo, Tanzania, Zambia, the Sudan, Benin, the Ivory Coast, Nigeria, Senegal, Guinea, Angola—fourteen African countries in all. He's toured in Europe and now lives in Brussels, Belgium. He finally made it to the United States in 1983 with the full T.P.O.K. jazz and two sets of dancers. African fans at the New York concert actually jumped up on the stage to get Polaroid photos of the giant figure with the minuscule guitar on his chest. But many New York fans were disappointed with the variety-show pacing of the evening. The dancers running on and off the stage kept the show from lagging. But they also kept Franco from doing many of his famous solo runs that are supposed to happen when the band abruptly changes gears and goes into a guitar-and-percussion-only break (a remnant of the *montuno,* or improvisatory, sections of Cuban music).

Having absorbed rock and disco influences of the 70s, soukous music today has gained new sounds and a clarity on record. But it also, in the mix, lost some of its rhythmic vitality. The disco thump is more prominent, and the sweet vocal harmonies are more up front, leaving a lot less emphasis on the intricate guitar work. But, generally, the most frequent criticism, and also one of the most amazing things about Zairian music, is that it doesn't change. "The music has become more commercial," says Richard Dick, who collected the material for Island Records' *Soukous* compilation. "But I wouldn't say the music has changed that much, [although] the albums are better recorded today."

One reason the music doesn't change much is the musical situation in Kinshasa. There are simply no instruments or other things necessary to form a band, such as microphones, available. The only musicians who have instruments are in existing bands, dominated by Rochereau's and Franco's groups. New stars must work their way through the two top bands.

There are, however, dynasties of rock-influenced bands that were founded in the 70s. Zaiko, for example, spawned Zaiko Langa Langa (which put out two of the top hits in Zaire last year, "Dallas Passport" and "Dynasty"), le Grand Zaiko, Zaiko Star, and Clan Langa Langa. Lita Bembo, an ex-singer with Franco, has formed a band called Stukas that uses drum machines and synthesizers with the web of guitar, keeping with trends in Western dance music.

Since 1972, there's been a growing roster of women singing stars to rise to high celebrity. In that year, Abeti Masikini broke the unwritten taboo against women getting up on a Congolese stage and created her own rhythm, the *sakossa*. She conquered the Olympia in Paris and Carnegie Hall in New York in 1974, gaining the title of "The Tigress" of Zaire. M'bilia Bel started out as a dancer with Masikini, and has become a huge seller in France, where she was recently voted number-one vocalist by Radio France International's Canal Tropical show. M'Pongo Love, the Golden Voice of Zaire, completes the trio of top female Zairians. In 1960, as a four-year-old child with the name of M'Pongo Landu, she came down with polio and was confined to a wheelchair. While working as a secretary for an auto dealer in Kinshasa, she frequently sang for friends; they convinced her to sing in public. Finally, in 1976, she toured East Africa and gained so much attention that she was invited to the FESTAC '77, the pan-African cultural festival held in Lagos, Nigeria. As a recording artist, she now writes many of her own songs, which are heavily tinged with highlife and calypso.

The artists who emigrated from Zaire in the 60s have developed their own blends of Congolese and highlife, with the ones that settled in Kenya and Tanzania dabbling in local beats such as the benga as well. These local beats make the music quicker, thicker, and to some ears, even more cheery. The most popular of the East

Tabu Ley Rochereau brings a crowd to its feet in Ouagadougou, Burkina Faso.

Billy Bergman

African expatriates is Mzee Makassy of Tanzania, whose Orchestra Makassy has recently released an album on Virgin Records, *Agwaya*. Makassy was born in East Zaire in the early 40s and while a teenager played bass in both Congolese and Western pop bands. During the turbulence of the 60s, he moved to Kampala, Uganda, where he played in the International hotel for many years. Idi Amin came to power in Uganda, and Makassy (who had formed his Orchestra in 1975) left to settle in Dar-es-Salaam, Tanzania. Constant touring in both Tanzania and Kenya has made him an East African celebrity today. But nothing has been easy for Makassy. His lead singer was stabbed to death in a street incident; as *Agwaya* was about to be recorded, the Tanzanian government decided that they owned the tapes if it was recorded in local studios, and so the whole operation had to be moved to Kenya. Finally completed in 1983, this, Makassy's first sophisticated recording, has gained the international attention his music deserves.

Other Congolese artists have found success even farther afield. Since 1963, Pamelo Mounk'a had been floundering in the highly competitive music world of Brazzaville and Kinshasa with about seventy records made in makeshift recording facilities headed by a local shopkeeper. Finally, he was discovered by Eddy'son Records in Paris, who invited him to come there at his own expense and co-produce a record. The result was the 1981 smash hit "L'Argent Appelle L'Argent" (Money Calls Money). The Kanda Bongo Man had seen some success in the Kinshasa youth scene when he teamed up with Soki Diazenza, who was the first musician to come on stage with a leopard-skin t-shirt. But Kanda was still working in factories to subsidize his music when he traveled to France and made some progress with "Lyole" and "Djessy," two marginal hits. A third European emigre, Fanfan, had come up through the ranks of Franco's O.K. Jazz before forming Somo Somo in the United Kingdom, backed by a group made up of British musicians he had taught to play in the Congolese style.

Even in these faraway places, the music serves as more than just a popular dance music for the locals. It has a function in a strange modern initiation rite for young Congolese men, as well. This rite is called "La Sape," and it is the art of dressing well in high-fashion clothing. The *sapeurs* are usually from Brazzaville, are from fifteen to twenty-five years of age, and belong to the Kongo ethnic group, who were the first from the region, they proudly claim, "to wear suit jackets." Without any possibility of employment in Brazzaville, they

M'Bilia Bel, protege of Rochereau, is a leading Zairian female vocalist.

Emanuel Bovet

A *sapeur* shows the important part of his tie in the ''Danse des Griffes'' in a Parisian club.

go to Paris to cultivate their look and win the admiration of their peers. The ultimate test of their status takes place on Saturday nights in elegant Congolese clubs around Paris where, to the recorded musical accompaniment of old Congolese favorite Papa Wemba, they compete in the "dance of the designer labels," during which they gracefully show the tags of their expensive outfits.

Meanwhile, back in Kinshasa, there are still not many instruments and microphones. And few people can afford to pay the entry fees to the discos where the musicians egg on the dancers with shouts of "Ambiance!" and "Ça bouge, non?," the rough equivalents of "Get in the groove" and "Shake that thing." But it doesn't matter. The people of Kinshasa dance in the streets outside the clubs and around the speakers of record shops, while Franco, Rochereau, and M'bilia Bel dance their soukous around the world.

DISCOGRAPHY

Various Artists	THE SOUND OF KINSHASA	Original Rec OMA 103
Various Artists	SOUND D'AFRIQUE II: SOUKOUS	Mango 9754, or Island ILPS 4008
Rochereau with Mbilia Bel	TABU LEY	Shanachie 43017
Franco and Rochereau	OMONA WAPI	Shanachie 43024
Franco	FRANCO ET TPOK JAZZ À PARIS	Makossa M2377
Orchestra Makassy	AGWAYA	Virgin V 2236
Pamelo Mounk'a	L'ARGENT APPELLE L'ARGENT	Eddy'son CM 636
Kanda Bongo Man	IYOLE	AR 00181
M'Pongo Love	FEMME-COMMERCANTE	Safari Ambiance 036
Somo Somo	SOMO SOMO	Sterns 1007
Nyboma	DOUBLE DOUBLE	Rounder 5010

NIGERIA

Lagos   Onitsha

Jak Kilby

AFRO-BEAT

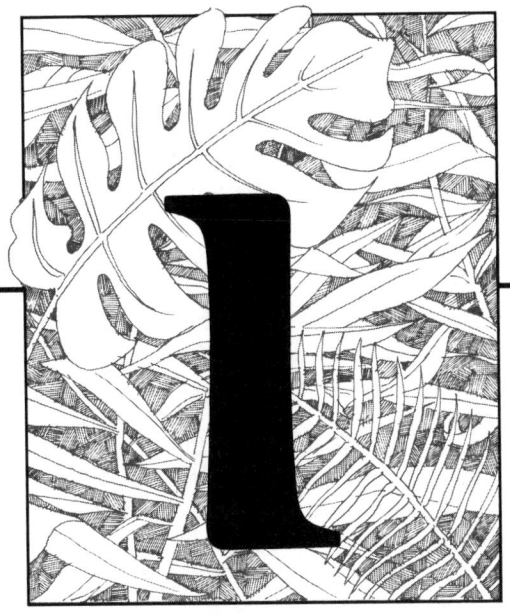

In Lagos, the sprawling, inoperative capital of the most populated country in black Africa, the atmosphere is a lot more serious than in the francaphone capitols that sway to rhumba. Though North American black music is popular all over Africa, it is here that common roots and attitudes have been able to mesh into new, truly African sounds. For example, the amplified beating of drums from a Fuji record playing at the record shop reverberates into a small, dark restaurant next door. Simultaneously, the teenagers who run the restaurant play Kool and the Gang at a slow speed on a radio-cassette player so the disco voices sound very similar to the Fuji talking drums. Three customers are huddled in the back near the air conditioner, sweating from the heavy, spicy foo-foo meal. One of the customers, the guitarist of an Afro-rock band, explains how much he loved the Beatles when he was younger, but the atmosphere is tense. The second customer, the manager of the band, has just found out that the band musicians have been negotiating on their own with the Paradise Lounge and are considering dumping him.

"I trusted you, and you stabbed me in the back," the manager interrupts. "That's what's wrong here in Nigeria," he says, turning to the third customer, who is a foreigner. "People do not know how to do business. They do what they want." The foreigner feels uncomfortable and looks over to a dark corner of the restaurant. Lightbulbs circle a mirror before a vanity, where a tall, striking girl carefully puts on makeup. "That's my fiancée," says the manager. "Isn't she beautiful?" This is the second woman today the manager has pointed out as his fiancée. One of the teenagers, very muscular in a sleeveless t-shirt, has been staring at the customers, and now

Fela Anikulapo Kuti on stage in London during a 1983 tour.

speaks to the foreigner. "May I ask your name?" he says. Then on hearing the reply, he mysteriously responds, "I would like to know you better than that." The lights go out and the teenager gets up to start a generator. "This is the third time in two hours," comes the band manager's voice from the dark.

The foreigner waits in the restaurant for the guitarist and the manager to accompany him to the Shrine, the nightclub of Fela Anikulapo Kuti, the King of Afro-beat. Tonight there is a concert to mark the seventh anniversary of Fela's Kalakuta Republic. But before they can go to the Shrine they must wait for the guitarist's girlfriend, who he has summoned through one of the teenager's younger sisters. After three hours, she appears, speaks a few words to the guitarist, and leaves. "Okay, we can go now," he says.

It's midnight and the streets are very quiet. People are afraid to go out; there are armed robbers around. Even if you're in a car, locals warn outsiders, they'll come over at a stoplight, order you out, and steal the car. A taxi is engaged to take the trio to Ikeja, the section of the city where Fela's Shrine is located. As he begins the trip, the driver informs them that he'll drop them at a crossroads near the club. The band manager verbally berates the driver. "This is what's wrong with Nigeria," he yells. "You have to fight with everybody. In New York, you tell a taxi where to go and he takes you there, right? That's his job. U'huhh. Here no one wants to do a job." The cab is stuck in a traffic jam—or a "go-slow" as they call it—on a wide street with shacks lining it: the taxi driver pulls up onto the sidewalk to pass by the congestion, descending into the road again to avoid hitting a sidewalk vendor. The taxi pulls alongside a Mercedes with two women in the back and the driver blasts the reggae song that is on the radio. The cause of the congestion, it turns out, is a military roadblock. "Good evening, brother," says a soldier to the taxi driver. He peers into the taxi and asks the foreigner "What's in the bag?" He looks in the foreigner's shoulder bag and sees a camera, which, the foreigner explains, he has because he is a tourist. "You're not a tourist," the soldier says. "There are no tourists in Nigeria."

After an exchange in Yoruba with the band manager, the soldier allows the taxi to continue. At the crossroads near the club, the trio disembarks from the taxi. The manager gives the driver only four naira—one less than the original bargain—because of the dropping-off point. They argue in Yoruba and the driver gives back the four naira. The manager quickly shoves the money back into his hand, along with three more naira. "What happened?" the foreigner asks. "He refused to take my money," replies the band manager. "That's bad juju. You can be dead in two days."

The dirt road leading to Fela's nightclub has ruts as deep as logs.

Claudia Thompson

Sonny Okosun (right) with Nigerian drummer Olatunji at S.O.B.'s in New York City.

The street is empty up to the very end, where there are lights, tables, cars, and a crowd of tough-looking young men and a few pretty girls in Western clothing. The long wall behind the crowd has two narrow doors and a box-office window. Entering through the second door, visitors are frisked by a small young man. The interior of the Shrine is huge, with a sea of folding chairs under a roofed area, a sunken area for dancing, and a large stage in the rear. Eleven musicians, a few wearing dark glasses, stand with their instruments at rest. In front of them, a tall young man in his early twenties harangues the members of the audience. The spirited discourse is in pidgin English, incomprehensible to the foreigner except for a few phrases here and there. "Africans have to take life more seriously.... If you give me shit, I'm gonna give you shit.... The struggle must stop.... There are no leaders in Africa." Audience members yell back, "O Kokoruku," or "Play music!" or "Stop talking." One man yells, "Like father like son!"

The tall young man is Femi, the son of Fela Kuti. He must go on talking, for his father has been temporarily silenced; in September of 1984 he was thrown in prison on a trumped-up charge of currency exportation. Fela is the only African musician who dares to continuously denounce the corruption of his own government and yet insists on living in his country. For this, he has been arrested innumerable times; he has been beaten seriously several times; he has had his residences wrecked repeatedly; his wives have been brutalized and raped; and his mother has been thrown out a window, from which she suffered injuries that led to her death.

Political criticism from musicians is rare in Africa, not only because it is dangerous under authoritarian regimes, but also because the place of a musician has never allowed it. Traditionally, musicians in Africa exist on the patronage of powerful figures, and this continues to be the rule today. As with the juju and griot musicians, praise singing is still a great part of the music-maker's function, and provides a large part of his income. Even in modern show-biz towns such as Abidjan, where singers focus more on variety than tradition, this patronage may exist. Aicha Kone, for example, a top female vocalist in the Ivory Coast, recently recorded a hit that told long-time president Felix Houphouet-Boigny what a wonderful guy he was and that the prosperity of the Ivory Coast was all the result of his efforts. The president, in turn, gave her a public birthday present of ten million local francs.

When musicians do venture to criticize politicians, it is often camouflaged in the complex system of double meanings in the African languages. "In Mandingo," says Ismail, the leader of the popular Senegalese group Toure Kunda, "I can tell you something and then I can say the same thing to four other people and they'll each understand something different. So many of our songs have political criticism and you can't tell." For example, this type of metaphor-couched criticism was used effectively in Rhodesia (now Zimbabwe) by such musicians as Thomas Mapfumo, to oppose the white minority regime that previously ruled.

But in general, performers feel their duty is to voice social rather than political criticism. Folktales set to music often have moral punchlines, telling how to behave in certain family situations, how to divide limited resources in hard times, how rituals should be followed, etc. Modern songs often decry the new morality that exists in the cities; faltering loyalty for economic gain is a favorite topic. One of the Lijadu Sisters, talented Afro-rock singers who often provide such social commentary, explains, "I'm an artist. I should not dabble in politics. We have always dealt in social problems because it's our problem and it continues. . . . Artists are in a better position to get through to people without hiring thugs. If people realize that our field is a means of correcting the society subtly, then more emphasis should be made on building the image of the artist. ...It's up to your manager to say look, you have to present a very good image when you go out; there are certain places you shouldn't go, certain things you shouldn't do. These are sacrifices I am prepared to make."

Criticism of attitudes and lifestyle has, in fact, become an ever-present theme in the day-to-day life of Lagosians who seem to be forever blaming each other—and themselves—for the disorganized state of things. There is a universal feeling that Nigeria has great potential, both economically and culturally, as well as a strong will to do things their own way and not with the parental guidance of their former colonial rulers (an easy out Nigerians often claim the Ivory Coast took advantage of). If only, they wish, their fellow citizens would get in line. "We don't drive like that in Nigeria!" one driver yells to another who is driving in the lane of opposing traffic in order to pass a traffic jam. The new military government harps on this theme as well; what's wrong with Nigeria, they say, is that there is a lack of personal discipline. So, they instituted a "War Against Indiscipline" campaign, which uses buttons, TV advertisements, and the death penalty to discourage bribery, petty smuggling, and black marketeering. "Will you support economic sabotage of our country, Nigeria? No way!" shouts a radio announcer.

But Fela's complaint is not with the way that ordinary Nigerians behave in order to survive in a rapidly-changing society. It's with the big plunderers, local and foreign, who are out to get all they can for themselves, the country be damned. And he concentrates on the Nigerians themselves who fall into that category, instead of writing songs condemning outside issues such as apartheid, which is one of the few political subjects that makes its way into the songs of other Africans. "Nigeria is worse than South Africa," he has said. "Here, we have blacks oppressing blacks."

Fela wasn't always so outspoken. In fact, until 1969 he was the leader of a highlife band for which he wrote a song called "Keep Nigeria One," supporting the government's efforts to crush Biafra. "I wasn't politically minded at all," he told journalist Carlos Moore. "I made my comments as a citizen. I was just another musician... singing love songs, songs about rain, songs about people..."

In 1938, Fela was born into a prominent Christian family, the Ransome-Kutis of Abeokuta. His father was the Reverend I.O. Ransome-Kuti, the principal and music teacher of a local primary school. He was a strict disciplinarian feared and admired by Fela because "he kicked everybody's ass" when they got out of line, even those of the British authorities. His mother, Funmilayo, was a political activist in the Nigerian Women's Union who, he claims, was the first woman in Nigeria to drive a car. She also led 50,000 women in a sit-in to stop the local chief from taxing market women, visited a number of Communist countries, met with Mao Tsetung, was a friend of Kwame Nkrumah of Ghana, and took Fela with her to political meetings when he was a boy.

In secondary school, Fela came out from under his father's domination and became more extroverted, taking on nicknames like Simon Templar and El Paso Kid. He formed a club called the Planless Society, several of whose members later became big cheeses in Lagos. The club had no rules except spontaneous disobedience. For instance, they would sneak Fela's mother's car and go nightclubbing in Lagos. During this period Fela met J.K. Braimah, a singer in Victor Olaiya's Cool Cats. J.K. came from a non-Christian, polygamous family and impressed Fela with his ability to chase women, drink, and smoke. "At that time, man," Fela told Moore, "there was nothing more popular in Nigeria than Ghanaian highlife. J.K. introduced me to Victor Olaiya and the Cool Cats and I began singing with them. J.K. got a kumba band together, with people like Godrich Khan, who is now a doctor...and we would go

Fela's son Femi leads Egypt '80 at the Shrine during his father's current imprisonment.

Billy Bergman

on the air. We were playing highlife and jazz on the radio, man!"

After graduating from high school, Fela tried working as a bu-
reaucrat in the government office of Commerce and Industries, but
left after six months. He got his mother to send him to Britain to
study classical music and theory, which he did seriously for four
years. During that time he met up with J.K., who was there studying to become a lawyer, and they decided to buy instruments and
form a highlife band called Koola Lobitos, which kept them in
pocket money and dandy clothing and at wild parties.

Before returning to Nigeria, Fela finished his studies, married his
first wife, and had children. He returned to Lagos in 1963, where he
continued playing with Koola Lobitos. The music was still highlife,
or highlife jazz, as he called it. Fela wrote all their tunes and played
both trumpet and saxophone.

Then, in 1966, funk music hit Nigeria in the form of Geraldo Pino,
a James Brown clone from Sierra Leone. "He came to town with
James Brown's music, singing, 'Hey, hey, I feel all right, ta, ta, ta,
ta.'...This man was tearing Lagos to pieces...he came in a big
way—in a convertible Pontiac....After that motherfucking Pino
tore up the scene, there wasn't shit I could do in Lagos....So we
went to Ghana. And one day in Accra we entered this club, Ringway
Hotel. The place was packed, man! Geraldo Pino was playing there.
Ohhhh, come and hear this music-o! See this guy's equipment!...
In Lagos, I was using this old equipment...museum antiques,
man. One microphone! This motherfucking Pino had six! The whole
place was jumping. The music carried me away completely. To me,
it was really swinging music. I say 'Look at the drummer, how he
play drums! This is heavy-o!'...I knew I had to get my shit together.
And quick!"

While other bands rushed to copy Pino's copy of James Brown,
Fela attempted to capture its excitement yet retain his African
identity. He wasn't quite sure what his music would be, but he
found a name for it—Afro-beat—formed a club called the Afro-spot,
and bribed the press to hype both. By now it was 1969, the Biafran
war was raging, and Koola Lobitos got an offer to go to the United
States. They took the offer and ended up in Los Angeles, strapped
for money and playing highlife for displaced Africans.

One night Koola Lobitos was hired to play at an NAACP function.
There Fela met and became involved with a young woman named
Sandra Smith, a member of the Black Panthers. Sandra introduced
Fela to the *Autobiography of Malcolm X*, Nikki Giovanni, The Last
Poets, Angela Davis, Martin Luther King, Stokely Carmichael, and
Jesse Jackson. For the first time, he recalls, he knew what it was to
be an African, and he wanted to create an African music. "In my

mind, I put a bass here . . . a piano there . . . then I started humming, then singing. I said to myself, 'How do Africans sing songs? They sing with chants. Now let me chant into this song: la-la-la-laaa . . .' " He remembered James Brown, whose music he realized was much more African than the imitations of Geraldo Pino.

The influence from James Brown should not, however, be thought of as one-way. As Koya, a member of the highlife band African Connection, says, "The first time I heard James Brown played in my village, I said, 'wow' because I could hear the guitars doing exactly the same things we played on the drums." But there might have been an even more direct influence from Fela to James Brown. There was an amazing change in Brown's music in the early 60s, away from soul ballads toward the relentless African repetitions of his later music. And at the time of this change, he supposedly had a sax player named Marco Parker, who had also played with Fela in Koola Lobitos. One of Brown's songs in the pivotal year of 1963, "Little Mother's Helper," also known as "I Feel Alright," bears a very strong resemblance to a 1959 African hit called "Manakoide" by a musician named Farka, no doubt a familiar tune to Parker.

Wherever the influences originated, they all came together very quickly for Koola Lobitos, knit by the drumming of seminal Afro-beat drummer Tony Allen. Fela introduced his "first African tune," "My Lady's Frustration," at the Citadel del Haiti on Sunset Boulevard and drove the crowd wild. His early Afro-beat songs display the full vitality of the form. A long introduction builds the rhythm section with polyrhythms and funk syncopations by the rhythm guitar, usually in minor chords with a good amount of sevenths and ninths. The horn section enters with startling unison, then keyboard riffs are added. Then Fela begins singing in his reedy voice backed by the unison call-and-response chanting of women. During the songs, there are solos by Fela and the other horn players that have a hint of jazz, but are simpler scales against one or two chords. The riffs repeat without letup for a good ten or fifteen minutes.

Things started happening very fast for Fela. EMI put out an album, *Fela's London Scene*, in 1970. An American producer had suggested the name Nigeria '70 for the group; Fela changed it to Africa '70 according to his newly acquired ideas of African identity, for Nigeria was a colonial creation. He attracted the attention of several Western rock musicians. Ginger Baker, the flamboyant drummer of Cream, was inspired to collaborate with Fela and subsequently brought the first well-equipped recording studio to Lagos. J.K. Braimah rejoined him as PR man, manager, and "everything." Together, Fela and Braimah turned the album *Shakara*, containing the all-time favorite "Lady," into a smash hit in 1972.

At first, Fela's Afro-beat music wasn't confrontational, but he himself was getting a lot of attention, and his lifestyle and critical attitudes were well-known. He set up an African-style commune in the middle of Lagos, which he eventually named the Kalakuta (rascal) Republic, after the name on his jail cell when he was arrested for the first time in 1974. "Ah-hah! What is this city shit-o? One man, one wife, one house isolated from everybody else in the neighborhood? Is an African not even to know his neighbors?" Scores of Fela's friends, relatives, musicians, and his many women began living within the concrete walls of Kalakuta. Dozens of other people—dispossessed youths, prominent Nigerians, Europeans, Ginger Baker—hung out there, talking, teasing each other, and smoking marijuana. The surrounding area became a sort of red-light district, with many small bars and a lot of black-market activity. "You should have seen it," says Nelson Tackie, who at the time was playing guitar for Sonny Okosun. "When he was going to play at the Shrine, across the street from Kalakuta, his boys would stop both lanes of traffic on Agege Motor Road, so that Fela and the women could walk across in their stage costumes and makeup."

During the heyday of Kalakuta, when he had money, Fela's life was riddled with contradictions that would horrify Western radicals. "He had so, so many cars," said one musician. "He loved getting the new ones when they came out." "He treated the women, whether they were his girlfriends or not, as slaves," said a local resident who claimed he went out with a girl who was one of Fela's singers; because of the date, he says, she was beaten and locked in a room. Whether or not the story is true, Fela has made numerous statements—about the subordinate condition of women, for example—that would drop the jaw of even the most sympathetic white liberal. The problem is, if Fela is a radical, he is a radical traditionalist, a world view that always has reactionary tints. He's not against ostentation; in traditional society it is the privilege and obligation of someone who has money to buy cars and spread money around.

Money also gives one the right to be heard. As Fela acknowledged in a later, less prosperous time, "I don't have the bread to push my ideas," but at this time he sang his opinions loudly. He did not protest against the existence of rich people, but against the covert siphoning of millions of Nigerian naira into Swiss bank accounts. He's not against authoritarianism; he's against weak leaders and strong men who have no ideology beyond personal gain.

Fela is most lucid when he relates his ideas as influenced by one leader he feels did have a great ideology, Ghanaian president from 1960 to '66, Kwame Nkrumah. Following Nkrumah's philosophy, Fela puts himself outside the *cause célèbre* of the moment to look at the whole African picture. "To raise money for a famine is nothing," he recently told French journalist Françoise Huguier in an interview conducted from, then smuggled out of, prison, "It's not the solution, because you can't keep raising for Ethiopia forever. There is famine in other places, too. It is a punishment for Africans because Nkrumah said Africa must have one government so that there can be free movement in Africa, free trade, planned agriculture, planned economy. If it was like that now there would be no famine in Ethiopia today. All Nkrumah's plans are true . . . but they don't want it because they want Africa to be divided so that Buhari's government can chop the money in Nigeria without having any problems with anybody else. . . . Every government can steal as much as they want to overseas banks . . ."

Since 1974, Fela has been under relentless persecution for such views. At first the pretext for arrests was possession of marijuana—which Fela made no secret of smoking—and then of kidnapping women—who actually come to him voluntarily, attracted to the man and the possibility of travel and money, or drawn to a commune in the city that reproduced the organization of the villages they came from. None of these charges stuck, though, for Fela has many friends both on the top and on the bottom. For instance, his cellmates once aided him to evacuate his bowels in secret while the police waited for the exit of some marijuana he had swallowed during a raid.

The raids and arrests only made Fela more vocal—his response to the above story was the song "Expensive Shit"—which made the police and soldiers more brutal, ransacking his house and beating him to within inches of his life. His song "Zombie," describing soldiers as mindless puppets of colonialism, became a worldwide hit. In his most daring protest he withdrew from the FESTAC pan-African cultural festival in early 1977 and held a counter festival at the Shrine, denouncing the abuses of the military and corrupt officials to the international audience that had come to Lagos. Fela was particularly enraged by "Operation Ease the Traffic," that had soldiers bearing horsewhips in the streets with orders to administer on-the-spot beatings to anyone, who, in their opinion, was contributing to the "go-slow."

The military waited until the festival was over to get back at Fela. After a couple of small skirmishes between soldiers and Fela's "boys," a force of one thousand soldiers surrounded Kalakuta. By now, the compound was a fortress, with electrified barbed wire crowning the concrete block walls and a heavily protected front gate. The soldiers blew up the electrical generator with heavy-weapons fire, broke down the gate, and went on a rampage. They

Onyeka, an Afro-Rock singer who narrated a British TV documentary about Lagos, Nigeria.

raped and brutalized the women, badly beat Fela and his brother, and broke their mother's leg by throwing her out a window. Gasoline was spread around and the Kalakuta Republic went up in flames.

Soon after this raid, Fela was exiled to Ghana. But the buoyant singer and his song "Zombie" were a hit there, and many students were eager to hear his ideas, which they found similar to those of Nkrumah. On his return to Nigeria, Fela married all twenty-seven of his women in a traditional ceremony, calling them, thereafter, his "queens." But his sorrows were renewed soon after, when his mother died, never having recovered from the Kalakuta horror.

The endless persecution has taken a toll on Fela and his music. "The first time I heard Fela," said a former producer of Fela's music, "I thought, 'that's the guy that's going to put Africa on the world map.' But he blew the whole thing... he went too political.... When Fela was Fela that was 'Jeun Ko'Ku,' that was 'Lady.' But... he talks more than actually singing these days... and the further [he] go[es], the more [he] lose[s] the African elements." His attacks on abuse of power and neo-colonialism have become even more blatant in songs such as "I.T.T. International Thief Thief" and "V.I.P. Vagabonds in Power," but the music has actually become flatter, losing some of the thrilling mesh of counterrhythms. His ability to play saxophone was severely impaired when his hands were crushed in a 1981 beating. He's lost some of his best musicians: Tony Allen, who wanted to have his own career, and many Ghanaian musicians who had to leave the country because of what Fela calls the "stupid, stupid, most treacherous and useless alien law" that cost Prince Nico his Cameroonians. The new Shrine, in an area of Lagos near the airport, is almost inaccessible in a city without night transportation, especially as thuggery has increased; others are afraid to go to the Shrine for fear of police raids.

So, in the years before Fela's jailing, concert attendance began to drop off sharply. And when "the Shrine is very dry like this you don't feel like blowing so much.... I don't work the band so much now," Fela said in 1983 to explain his band's lack of tightness. Just prior to this, his manager, Martin Messonier, a Frenchman very active on the Nigerian music scene, abruptly dropped Fela to work with Sunny Adé and Island Records. Record royalties to Fela had slowed drastically, and he was broke. His wives began to leave him.

Fela could have averted many of his problems and continued voicing his opinions openly if he had left Nigeria. "I can't leave my country," he countered. "That's my problem.... Many Africans leave to be heard, but I can't be a first-rate musician from a fourth-rate country. I will never leave home for more than two months." And even if his situation was bad, he was biding his time, waiting

Juliet Highet

Geraldo Pino from Sierra Leone helped fuel the James Brown rage throughout Africa.

Members of Ghetto Blaster on the deck of their barge in the Seine.

for things to come together. "The African mind is cool. I'm content
with what I am," he said. He had recently found a new contentment
and a quiet power through the teachings of Professor Hindu of
Ghana. Besides performing such tricks as cutting a man's throat
and then reviving him, Professor Hindu explained to Fela his connections with the power of the African land and made Fela feel the
real significance of the name Fela Anikulapo Kuti, which means:
"He who emanates greatness, who has death inside his quiver, and

who cannot be killed by human entity." So Fela performed various Yoruba ceremonies at the Shrine and remained confident.

Things began to get better. Fela completed a successful European tour, which was to be followed by an American one in late August, 1974. It was to be his first U.S. tour since his Koola Lobitos days, and there was great anticipation, with large venues booked across the country. Then the harrassment started; exit visas were stalled and large New York gigs had to be postponed. Finally, the group members were given visas to leave. As the wives, musicians, and crew boarded the plane, Fela was arrested for having 1,600 British pounds on his person. Later, the Army Chief of Staff allegedly said he would "make sure Fela is jailed . . . and I hope he will rot in jail."

Meanwhile, the band (now called Egypt '80) arrived in the U.S. What could have been a triumph ended in a one-night stand at Pizza A-Go-Go, the only place in New York that the group, now led by Femi, could get a booking on a short notice. It got later and later, and the manager would still not agree on a fee. Some queens were dancing to avoid putting their costumes on; others sat sullenly, in full makeup, near the pizza counter. When the group finally went on at one A.M., the soundman decided to demand more money, cutting off the system numerous times. Afterwards, Femi railed against the United States to a few journalists in a small room downstairs, while a guitar player said, "I just want to go home."

Meanwhile, other Nigerian musicians today emulate Fela's achievements in creating new African music using elements of rock and rhythm 'n' blues. All these efforts come under the rubric Afro-rock. Sonny Okosun is currently the most successful in this vein, but most of his songs sound like fusions between highlife, reggae, rock, and akwete rhythms. "I really want to create a kind of beat which when you hear it, you know it is Sonny Okosun," he says. "Fela did it and Fela succeeded. We couldn't copy Fela . . . people are blind, they would just say, he's copying Fela and . . . nobody will listen to it. We decided to delve in from one song to another, we're trying to find out what to do. 'No More War' . . . was the first in my own Ozzidi style, leading up to 'Togetherness.' "

Okosun, nearly a decade younger than Fela, was weaned more on rock than on highlife. In fact, his inspiration to make music, he says, came from Elvis Presley movies. "I saw him with fans," he says, "and I thought they were his friends, you see. And I said to myself, 'If you want to have many friends, you have to go into music.' And that's when I found it necessary to learn the guitar. That was about 1963–'64." He learned guitar by playing Elvis numbers, then formed his first group, which played Beatles songs as well. He left his native Enugu, an Ibo area, during the Biafran war and came to Lagos, where he worked at the television station as a designer and played in amateur groups at the time James Brown and Otis Redding became popular. In 1969, Okosun joined Victor Uwaifo's band, then left the group after they toured Japan, stopping in England on his way home to pick up some cheap used instruments. These instruments became the foundation for his group, Ozzidi, named after a legendary hero. Since 1974, Okosun has put out about fifteen albums, nine of which have gone gold. He began Ozzidi with Afro-reggae fusions, from the first song, called "Help." ("I was seriously Beatles inclined and so inspired by the Beatles that I wanted to use all the Beatles titles. I got halfway and stopped.")

Okosun had a big political hit in 1976 with the song "Fire in Soweto," about the massacre of blacks in the Soweto township of South Africa. However, he finds the consequences of dealing with politics very frustrating: EMI wouldn't release him on their main label; a local newspaper said he was capitalizing on the problems of South Africa; a Pretoria journalist asked if he was being paid to sing about it by the Nigerian government. Lately, his hits have softer themes: the love between "Mother and Child" and the "Togetherness" between generations, though "Revolution" speaks of the yearnings of the young. Unfortunately, the demand for reggae "is dying down and...that is the music that gives us space to talk when we want to talk." But at least one of Okosun's dreams has come true: in 1984, he packed the Apollo Theater in New York's Harlem.

But preserving the full vitality of Fela's original Afro-beat, with its brilliant bass repetitions, tight horn sections, insistent chanting, and knit-together drumming, is a group of seasoned young musicians known as Ghetto Blaster. The group was formed in 1983 in Lagos and includes ex-members of both Fela's and Okosun's groups. Two French filmmakers, who were tired of New York and wanted an African adventure, drove down to Nigeria through the Sahara with film equipment, sold their Peugeot, and put together the group for a film script titled *Ghetto Blaster*. After the film, the band played dance nights at the Black Pussycat Club in Lagos, then was taken to several French music festivals. Parisian club dates followed, as well as tours with Archie Shepp, Manu Dibango, Xalam, Fela, and even James Brown. The Ghetto Blasters now float in the Seine on a barge that is their living space and rehearsal hall, waiting anxiously to see if their new 45 on Island Records will bring them an African or even an American tour.

Meanwhile, Fela is serving a five-year term in Lagos' Kirikiri Prison. Femi leads the band, which plays sporadically at the Shrine and still has some good horn players, who trade solos often now in concerts. Some of Fela's wives, who are dispersed throughout the city, come to sing, or to dance languidly in the fishnet go-go cages at the four corners of the Shrine's dance floor, dressed in evening gowns. Attendance at the Shrine is low. As one of the wives said, "There is no enjoyment here since Fela is put in jail." But there's no doubt he'll be back as strong as ever. Celluloid Records, with producer Bill Laswell, recently put out a new Fela album of material from pre-existing tapes. It is doing well in the U.S. and Europe. And a teenager, pointing to a huge stadium in the center of Lagos, says that it's rarely used because it's so big that no event could fill it. Then he adds, slyly, "except maybe the return of Fela."

D I S C O G R A P H Y

Fela Anikulapo Kuti and Afrika '70	SHAKARA	EMI 006 N, or EMI EDP 1547203
Fela Anikulapo Kuti and Afrika '70	ZOMBIE	Phonogram/Creole 511, or EMI EDP 1547203
Fela Anikulapo Kuti and Afrika '70	ORIGINAL SUFFERHEAD	Arista/Spart 1177
Tony Allen	NEEPA	Earthworks MWKS 3001
Lijadu Sisters	DOUBLE TROUBLE	Shanachie 43020
Onyeka	TRINA FOUR (HIGHLAND TOWN)	Sterns MAS 1201
Sonny Okosun	FIRE IN SOWETO	OTI LP 58
Sonny Okosun	WHICH WAY NIGERIA	Jive/Arista UIP 18
Sonny Okosun	LIBERATION	Shanachie 43019
Ghetto Blaster	"PREACHER MAN"/"EFI OGUNLE"	Island 880 344-1

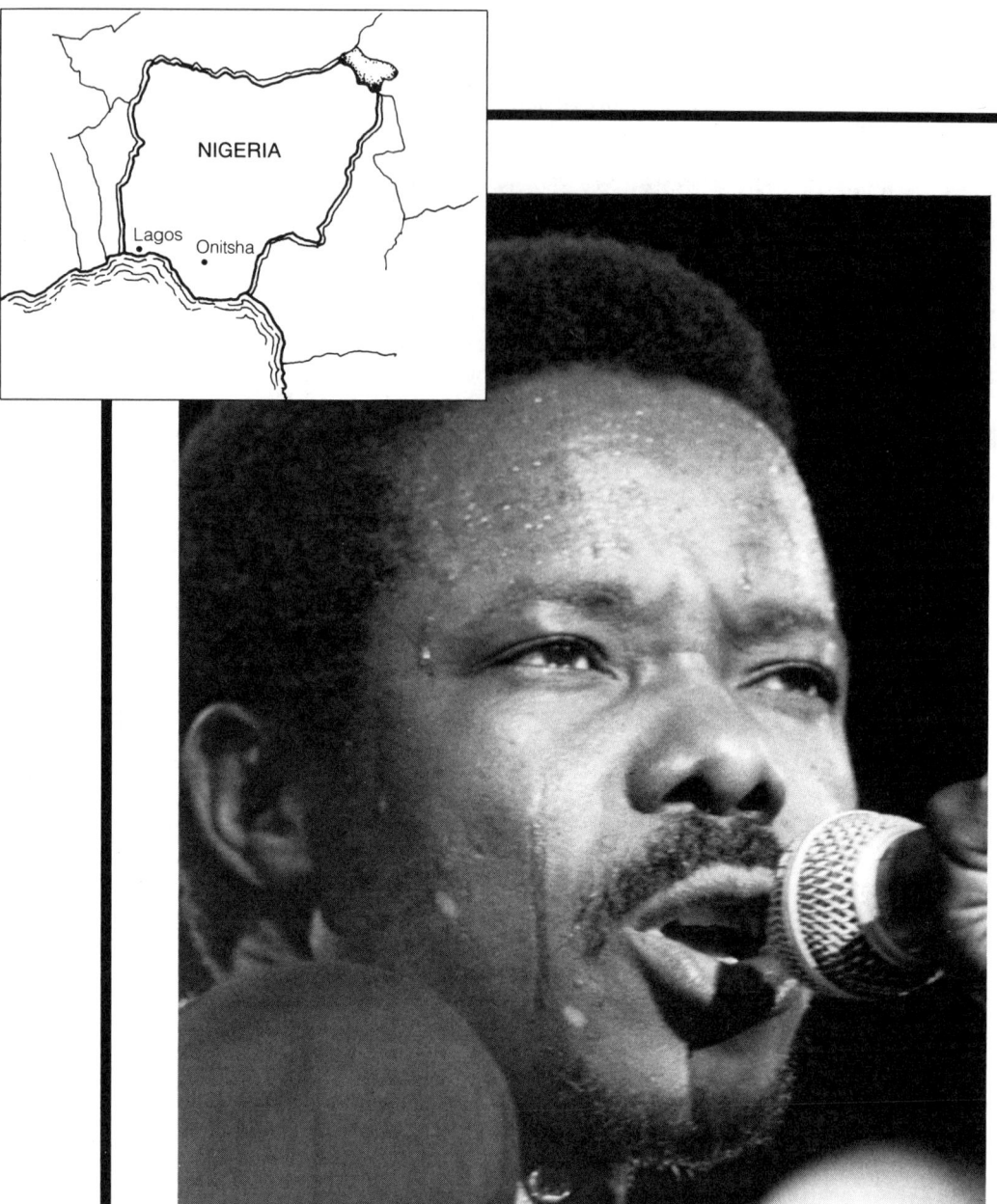

Claudia Thompson

NIGERIA

Lagos Onitsha

JUJU

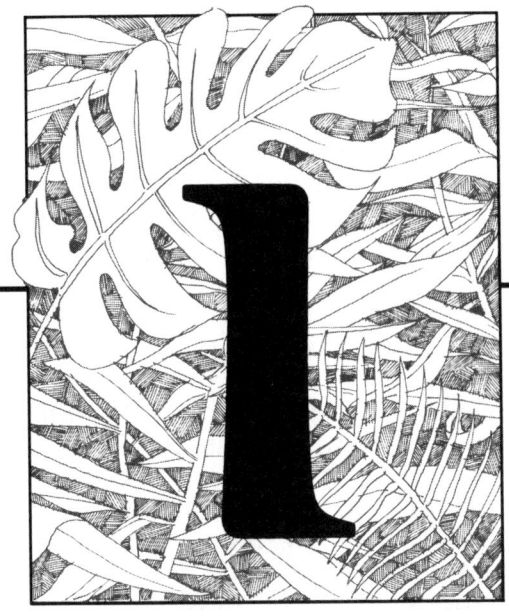

Chapter · Five

In 1983, two years after the death of reggae superstar Bob Marley, the international press heralded the arrival of the new ruler of world popular music. New Yorkers reacted to King Sunny Adé's first U.S. concert with awe and delirium. A music critic for *The New York Times*, Robert Palmer, overheard someone asking Chris Blackwell, the head of Island Records (which had just released the first Adé record aimed at a Western audience) whether he thought Adé would, in fact, become the next Marley. "Blackwell was so overcome by [Adé's] performance he could only nod his head mutely," Palmer recounts.

"It's important that we have people hooked on Sunny. We want to develop him as a cult figure for now. King Sunny Adé playing juju music is a great name and it is very easy for me to sell... great package," Martin Messonier, Adé's manager and producer for the Island album, explained to writer Robert Blau. Later, a publicist told Blau, "Channel 7 is coming down to the show tonight.... We've got *Life* magazine preparing a six-page spread... a *People* profile... this is beyond you guys in the music press. It's... it's a phenomenon." And indeed, Adé and his African Beats continued to reap accolades and sell out venues around the world. He was greeted by mayors, and he jammed with Stevie Wonder. The Western world loved the music so much, it seemed, that soon, Adé's primary juju rival in Nigeria, Chief Commander Ebenezer Obey, was signed by Virgin Records and began preparing his own assault on Europe.

Two years later, however, the fanfare has died down. Island dropped Sunny Adé after two albums for sales were not up to the expectations of rock labels. His tours, though still well-attended, have not yet attained stadium-level popularity or even been profit-

King Sunny Adé: not Bob Marley, but he holds a solid position in a strong culture.

able. His disappointed musicians, nineteen-year veterans who made up the African Beats, started bickering about money. The situation came to a head in Tokyo, Japan, in 1984. The band had been invited to play in a charity concert to raise money for famine-stricken countries in Africa. The musicians decided to settle their complaints there and then, in the hotel before the concert. "It was a big disgrace," said Adé, "calculated to hold me to ransom." It was also the end of the African Beats.

But in Nigeria Sunny Adé has few problems. He's not only Amulu-dun (a traditional royal title) of Ondo and Amuludun of Lagos by birth, and Master Guitarist, Minister of Enjoyment, and Thunder Wire by general acclaim, he's also an institution. He quickly reconstituted his band from irregulars in the group (his fifty-two-man group included twenty regular members, with about twenty-two playing at any one time) and gave it a new name, The Golden Mercury of Africa, after another honor that had once been bestowed on him. Soon he announced the launching of his "new outfit" with a motorcade that visited all the top media in Lagos. At the Lagos *Daily Times,* Adé was met by Chief Funsho Akindele, who praised him effusively, saying that "it isn't politicians or people in government alone that make a country thick, known, and respectable," citing as examples Pelé of Brazil and Mohammed Ali of the U.S. He voiced his pleasure at seeing "Sunny Adé Live in Switzerland" on British television, then continued, "I felt happy and proud. You have made a name for Nigerians and Africans as well. Your success is our success and we wish you every bit of luck with your new outfit."

A couple of weeks later, Adé debuted the Golden Mercury of Africa at his club, Ariya, in the center of Lagos. The place was packed by midnight, and outside huge bouncers fought excitedly about whether to bring in more chairs and tables. Inside, it was as if this was the same band. Squeezed onto the tiny stage, the group of twenty-two musicians, nearly one-half percussionists, with the other half comprised of four electric guitars, a bass, a steel pedal guitar, a synthesizer, and jubilantly dancing singers, was as tight as ever. Throughout the two to three-hour non-stop sets, Adé only waved his guitar or stomped his foot to signal abrupt changes to the twenty-odd member group, and they were able to follow improvisations as if they had been rehearsed. At one point, when the only white person in the audience stepped forward to take a picture of him, the King began a verse that started with "psychedelic photographer," and as he continued singing in Yoruba, the chorus harmonized "Hamburger, Coca-Cola."

In the back of the club, which is divided by a sunken, thatch-roofed pavilion with tables underneath, the atmosphere was highly charged even at two o'clock in the morning—a result of the non-stop music and the drinking to which thousands of empty beer bottles on the tables attested. The audience shouted greetings and teasings. A man returned to his seat after dancing and found it had been taken by someone else; he roared, "Get up!" and cursed in Yoruba until others began admonishing him. Musicians, including some of the ex-African Beats, hustled connections.

At the other end of the club, in front of the tiny stage holding twenty-two musicians, the action was hot and heavy. The dance floor was constantly packed with a majority of the audience, who rotated their shoulders while they crouched down. The spectators ranged from late twenties to mid-fifties in age, and were dressed, for the most part, in traditional robes. The stage was elevated less than a foot above the dance floor, so the audience members were easily able to show their appreciation by stepping up and pasting naira notes on Adé's forehead or touching them to his forehead and stuffing them into the pocket of his brilliant white suit. Adé beamed. The talking drums bubbled and thundered, the steel pedal guitar and synthesizer wafted in and out. Adé, cool and relaxed, added quick guitar bursts or long surf-music lines whenever he felt like it, while high-pitched metal knockers and shakers kept a constant clave-like beat. The pace rolled hour after hour.

Projecting from the right side of the stage was a sort of VIP section, tables filled with middle-aged, distinguished-looking men and women who smiled when Adé mentioned their names in his sung praises. A Mediterranean businessman, dressed in a suit, waited for a short break in the music to hand Adé a large check.

Juju music, which became popular at about the same time that American soul music and American black pride were helping Fela to find his roots, has several traditional functions within modern Yoruba society. Therefore, the music is strongly supported in Lagos, which despite its apparent disorder, has a very strong Yoruba substructure; it is dominated by this one ethnic group.

As opposed to many other large cities in Africa, where lingua franca are used for everyday communication, the streets of Lagos are awash with the lulling tones of Yoruba. A fender-bender accident in the narrow streets of Lagos causes the air to fill with shouted Yoruba as the two drivers concerned, the drivers stuck behind the accident, and all the market vendors take sides in a grand debate. Many of these people wear traditional flowing robes and head wraps. Even young people sport the facial scars that indicate particular subgroups; most of them are aware of the region that they, or their parents, came from, and their relationship, if any, to the local traditional rulers. Many of these rulers now have high positions in business or government agencies, and they form a strong network among themselves, evident in the pages and pages of congratulatory notices in the back of Nigerian newspapers.

One reason for this cohesiveness is that the Yoruba-speaking area, for at least 1,000 years before the twentieth century, was organized into a system of city-states; the original seven were Oyo, Ketu, Owu, Benin, Ila, Sabes, and Ake, many of which exist as regions today. The Kingdom of Oyo eventually conquered the other six cities and brought them together in one large empire. The unity between these cities was disrupted by wars and the incursions of Islam and the Europeans. So, a complex system of local rulers developed to govern each area, retaining the palaces and the courtly ambiance. An important part of this ambiance was music, which varied from area to area but had universal functions: the celebration of certain events, such as the installation of a new chief, births, deaths, weddings; the education in traditional values; and the praise of great men. Tonal drums—called talking drums—were a large part of this music and were used for communication as well.

When highlife swept Nigeria in the late 50s, it seemed that a parallel music to fill the needs of the modern, urban-centered environment of Yoruba had not yet developed. But by 1968, such a music *had* developed, pressed by an important need. In that year, the winning soccer team—the Stationery Stores—needed to be praised. A song, lauding them with words, talking drums, and guitars, sold an amazing 500,000 copies. From that moment on, juju music had a solid place in Yoruba society. And the song's performer, Sunny Adé, had gained a lifelong niche on top of Nigeria's—and eventually the world's—music scene.

Juju's origins are obscure. "Juju music, way back in the early 20s, was built up from the music played in shrines," claims Adé. "They centralized it so that it doesn't have anything to do with any religion or any shrine today." According to Adé, the distinguishing feature of the music back then was a percussion unit called *gangan*, which contained the core rhythms that exist in juju to this day.

In the 40s, a man named Tunde Nightingale garnered popular attention playing exotic party music in the Yoruba areas of Western Nigeria. The music was exotic because it didn't sound very Yoruba in its rhythm and instrumentation. So, it was given the not-so-serious name of juju, after the sound of the drum (jujuku) or the word for "magic" in some pidgin usage. Nightingale's ensemble included a ukulele, a banjo, and a samba—a little square drum with obvious connections to the ones played in Brazil. At the same time, a music called *kokoma* was developing in the area around Lagos, possibly related to the konkomba music that developed from the

Jak Kilby

A Nigerian drumming troupe playing in a park in London.

coast brass band music spreading inland. Usually kokoma used three drums, a large Yoruba hand piano, and a large chorus of voices. Other types of new ensembles were forming at the time, some using a large wooden box as a main percussion instrument. At some point, these talking drums were included in kokoma.

Up until the late 50s, this was all music for lower classes and village dwellers, according to highlife expert John Collins. In 1960, however, I.K. Dairo formed the first well-known juju dance band. To make the band and its music an integral part of Yoruba society, Dairo reinforced traditional values, especially in the lyrics and the singing, which featured the characteristic Yoruba harmonies. He enriched the music with epigrams—"incantations, verses, and expressions"—which he researched, he told writer John Storm Roberts, by traveling around, "talking to old men who know a lot about such things: I then go home and turn them into modern music." And for modern appeal, "what I usually do is to concentrate more on the rhythm, the time, and most of all, the beat. . . . To make my music appeal, I have introduced various beats and tempos to suit the different tribes."

Dairo's modernizations attracted young devotees. "That was the music I loved most," says Adé. He developed juju by putting a guitar into it, and also by introducing the accordion and the big talking drum. The accordion is not used much in juju anymore, but the booming and babbling of the talking drums have become its most distinguishing feature. The talking drum, as the name implies, actually communicates. It "talks," not through any kind of Morse Code, as early explorers in Africa assumed, but by imitating local speech. This is possible because of the tonal nature of the languages spoken in the regions where talking drums are played. The pitch goes up and down, in the drumming, following the pattern of speech in a certain phrase. Traditionally, the talking drum was used to send messages from village to village, as well as to summon people to a certain place in one village. In music, it was employed to praise a powerful person, to celebrate a joyous occasion, or to supply another layer of lyrics to various kinds of music.

In juju, the talking drum used is a *dondon*, an hourglass-shaped, two-headed drum held under one arm and beaten with a crooked stick. The drum heads are held in tension by leather thongs, and the pitch is raised by squeezing these thongs. Other articulate tones are achieved by hitting the head nearer to or farther from the rim, or by stopping the stick on the head instead of letting it bounce off after a strike. Of course, besides articulating phrases that have meaning, the dondons are also used for purely ornamental, musical phrases.

Since the 60s, and the establishment of a basic framework of percussion and guitars in juju bands, a major competition has developed between top juju stars to introduce new instruments to their sound. "In my production," says Chief Commander Ebenezer Obey, "I always add new thing[s] whenever I'm producing a new album. Not only in my production, but even on the stage. Here, people don't want to continue to eat the same type of food all the time. They need a change, and for that, it's important to introduce new instruments." But this is not just a matter of throwing in anything. "You see," says Obey, "it's very interesting trying to introduce new instruments and making sure they're accepted." There is nothing gimmicky about juju music; any new additions have to fit into the mesh of rhythms. The sound may be enriched, but nothing can stand out too much.

It's not always clear who introduced what to the music. "I started bass guitar," says Ebenezer Obey. "And I introduced two more guitars. And then the pedal steel guitar...coming to the state we have at the moment."

"I was the first to introduce...pedal steel guitar," counters Sunny Adé. "In 1976, I recorded it in Randall's Studio [in London] and took it back to Nigeria. Nobody knows how the pedal steel is, when I first brought it. The only steel guitar was with Bobby Benson musical show and Bobby gave it to me. I am confidently in the position to say that . . . introducing the pedal steel guitar, my band was the first one. Introducing the vibraphone, my band was the first one. Introducing the drum kit [the Western drum set], my band was the first one. Introducing multiple guitars, it was Ebenezer Obey who introduced the second guitar after Tunde Nightingale. It was I.K. Dairo who introduced accordion. I was the first one to electrify the talking drums when I'm playing on the stage. I was the first one to use the two talking drums together."

Admiral Dele Abiodun, a rising star on the juju scene, also has his claims to fame. "I started using the steel guitar—I started it," he says. "In 1974, in London, I decided I needed some sort of new thing. I took a guy off solo guitar and took him to the music store in London where he trained on steel guitar for two months. . . . The young man who started playing it with me at that time—may his soul rest in peace, he's dead now—he left my band and went to Ebenezer Obey as steel guitarist."

It should come as no surprise, by now, that juju musicians hear and want to incorporate these Western instruments into their music. Country-and-western records with the steel pedal sound, for example, were promoted in Nigeria by multinational record companies most heavily in the mid-70s. Jim Reeves, Don Williams, and Dolly Parton became very popular at that time. Electric guitars were ubiquitous, and by 1960, the Zairians had shown all of Africa that the guitars could be played in very African ways. The first one was probably brought to Nigeria by trend-setting bandleader Bobby Benson; for a long time in highlife the electrics used were either hollow-bodied or acoustic guitars with pickups.

Generally, the juju guitar style incorporates the bell-like legato of Zairian guitar into short phrases and rolling patterns. But each band has, in addition, individual guitar quirks that often relate more closely to rock and jazz than to Zairian guitar. Adé often features a rhythm guitar that resembles the one used in Afro-beat and funk, and when he solos, he sometimes goes for quick bursts and bent notes, as well as mellow, sustained phrases reminiscent of surf rock. Obey often has one guitar soloist who stands out from the rhythmic mesh through a whole number, playing lyrical jazz lines. There's a lot going on in the guitar section, but it's doubtful that all six players are needed. Many Nigerians, too, are skeptical when asked if they can actually hear all the guitar lines. "I think it is just a show," is a very common response. It is true that prestige and appearance are very important to juju bands and that instrumentalists come cheap. If the band is hired to honor a person or occasion, six electric guitars do more honor than four. But, whether or not all those musicians are used or needed all the time, juju music has broken ground with coordinated, polyrhythmic guitar playing.

Despite the constant stylistic and instrumental innovations, juju music remains firmly embedded in its traditional roles. "We use it to teach, we use it to educate," says Sunny Adé. "It is not all entertainment alone, because when you play juju music you are playing traditional music that has been around for decades, being refined. We play music when we want to entertain, we play it when it is a sorrowful time, we play in wartime, we play when we want to communicate."

For general education, juju uses the type of epigram that I.K. Dairo researched when he plumbed the wisdom of old men in the villages. This is mixed with Christian morality, since most juju musicians are Christians; Ebenezer Obey, for one, is quite religious. Practical advice and support for laudable government programs may also enter the lyrics. Obey put out a song reminding people to drive on the right-hand side of the road when Nigeria switched from the English traffic system; in his recent album, *Solution,* he supports the new government's "War Against Indiscipline" with the lyrics "Let us be orderly. Orderliness is everything." Adé tends to be more philosophical and prayerful, as in the song "Ja Fun Mi" or "Head [God] Fight for Me."

As praise singers, juju musicians fit well into the traditional mold. They praise patrons or "someone who is doing good things for the society or . . . a renowned person," says Adé, "an artist or footballer [soccer player] or a wrestler or someone who makes the country proud in some way." Younger artists are starting to get away from this function, however. "I don't get myself involved in praises," says Dele Abiodun. "I don't believe in it. Maybe I do it once every forty-two months." Segun Adewale, the most successful juju artist under thirty years of age, keeps away from praise-singing for practical reasons. "In the year 1982," he told writer Chris May in London, "I sing in praise of a company that say I should help promote their plastic coolers. They paid me some money and I did. But no more. I won't do it again. Let's have it that your name is John. Let's have it that someone is sitting behind you named Paul. You are my fan and you do so much for me but I sing in praise of Paul. You will not buy my record. . . . To be on the safe side, I will avoid it."

Praise, entertainment, and education all come together when juju bands play at occasions that, in Yoruba tradition, require music. These include installations of tribal royalty, weddings, births, and funerals. "If an old man dies," says Ebenezer Obey, "it is the belief

Jak Kilby

Prince Segun Adewale ''kick starts'' one of his yo-pop juju songs.

of the Yoruba people that the children of the deceased are happy to see the family tree kept on by themselves and they see it as good luck that they are not leaving before their parents. Traditionally, it calls for joy. We have musicians playing to rejoice with the family."

The most lavish celebrations accompanied by juju are the installations of a new village chieftain (oba). Bob George, a record producer from New York, accompanied Ebenezer Obey to one such function.

"This is the entrance to the BIG party—the installation of a new chief, the Oba of Ondo. I stand near the outbuildings and take it all in. Chief Obey nods toward the six or seven cattle tethered near the entrance and says, 'At my father's installation there were twenty-six cows!' The band laughs, and we all move towards the stage.

"Once past the cookhouse, the compound opens up into a plain about the size of a soccer field. At the far end is the elevated stage. Ranged around the edges of this clearing are tables and chairs, each table reserved with a namecard, the tables closest to the stage covered with a canopy. Overhead, zig-zagging strings of lights link the sides of the field. The bare bulbs alternate with pendants bearing photos of the Chief-to-be and his symbol, a rearing elephant.

"The pendants... are just the beginning of a PR blitz.... T-shirts, handed out to guests as they arrive, also bear the image of the Chief and the legend 'Congratulations Chief Akinsipe, the Oba of Ondo.' There are plastic mugs, napkins, towels, tall mixed-drink glasses, frisbees, and dinner plates—even souvenir programs and umbrellas for the musicians.... Food and drink is provided free to all....

"Many of the townspeople are gathering around the stage, watching the band set up and trying to get near Obey.... Hired guards patrol the stage area and swing burlap bags and long switches to keep 'fans' away. They do this throughout the night, and at some points it even seems necessary. About ten members of the regular police force, armed with billies, guard the perimeter.

"It's now about ten P.M.... As people take their seats the various hues that were a crowd now merge to form blocks of the same color. Each color defines one of the social clubs that make up 'High Society' in Ondo—chunks of blue, pink, brown, green, and white. About 400 men and women are all wearing variations of the same silk brocade patterned with the Oba's elephant symbol.

"After a long, sonorous, Apala-style praise song the celebration officially begins! Chief Obey takes the stage and launches into a praise song of his own. 'A, A is for Apple/K, K is for...' spelling out the name of their host. It's a [charming] set piece adapted to seem specially composed for the occasion.

"Obey's band, the Inter-Reformers, are fifteen strong.... The band is all in khaki—sort of vaguely military outfits with epaulets. The Chief is wearing a gold Givenchy shirt, hanging out over doubleknit trousers. Chief Obey is handed a sheet listing the various social groups and the order he is to call them up to dance. The Oba's table is first. They are dressed in white silk covered with silvery elephants. Only gold jewelry is worn tonight. One woman's headdress is six meters of heavy silk brocade woven in a pattern [made up of the words] 'Various Worldwide Passenger Aircraft.'

"After about twenty minutes the rest of the 'royal family' is invited to dance. The thick, prosperous bodies move cool to the juju [music]—Obey's 'miliki' beat...Yoruba for 'enjoyment.' It is the right sound for tonight.

"Soon the 'dashing' begins. 'Dashing' or 'spraying' is the custom of laying money on the head of someone you wish to honor. Often it is a hierarchical duty and a ritualized sign of respect. Sometimes you do it because you like a person. Sometimes it's a way to get noticed, a bribe, the repaying for a favor, or a way to show how successful you've become. Yoruba society demands proof of the status you claim and the power you wield. 'Dashing' is a part of that. Someone lays a flurry of large notes on [another person], and both giver and receiver gain stature. The 'ordinary' people in the crowd, seeing more money than they could ever hope to earn in their lifetimes, let out an audible 'aahh.'

"The top social club, the one that the Oba is the president of, hears its name. They are all in pale, shimmering pink. The elephants are blue. Throughout the night Chief Obey moves through the list: 'The Circle Z Club,' 'Club 75,' 'The Seven Sisters.' Each new name he calls brings out a different set of colors. No one dances out of turn, and as each club takes over the dance area they are joined for a while by the Oba and his wife. They mingle with the dancers, talk, get dashed, and dash.

"Of course, Chief Obey can hardly move while being smothered in naira! I never considered the logistics of excessive 'dashing,' but Chief Obey has. The stick player stands on a large wooden chest behind the Chief and peels the banknotes off the musicians' perspiring foreheads as fast as the guests apply them. When he can no longer hold them all, he jumps down, lifts the lid and stuffs the cash inside. In one motion he's back on the top of the box. The Chief is playing hard—singing the praises of the Oba and his guests. He pulls in about [3,000 naira].

"I soon realize that I have no social standing and am not, officially, allowed to dance. I'm saved by the stage hands and some of the native dancers, who invite me behind the stage with them. Here,

On one of his U.S. tours, Sunny Adé is "dashed" with dollar bills.

hidden from the view of the honored guests, is an impromptu 'workers' party. Even the policemen dance.

"This 'non-dancer' status applies to most of the people in the town. For this reason the Oba has set up another clearing, across the street, with another band. The artist is an up-and-coming juju star, Hansome Wale Abioden and His Black Beatles.

"About three A.M. [the lead singer] develops a leg cramp and comes crashing down on the stage. This is the occasion for the first break of the night. The Chief Commander and his band have played for four hours straight, and got through more than half of the list of social clubs. Soon, they start up again and continue until dawn."

Although Sunny Adé has estimated that there are more than 1,000 juju bands performing at clubs and ceremonies throughout Nigeria, there is room for very few at the top—in fact only two: Adé and Obey. They are the prestige performers, booked over a year in advance for important events. These two juju superstars were the obvious choices for the first international recording contracts.

Of the two, Obey is older; he was born in Idogo, Western Nigeria, in 1942. His interest in music was sparked by church choral singing and the school band. He began his own musical career at the age of twelve, while still in primary school. With several other students he formed a band called the Ifelode Mambo Orchestra, and they performed in the market and at parties on weekends. They played a local form of highlife called Agidebo music, which used a small zither, as well as kokoma music.

In primary school, too, Obey adopted his curious name. "You see, in those days, when I went to school, [the teacher punished the children]...whip!...and cut the skin. And the teacher say, 'If any person want to resist, well, obey first, and then complain.' " In other words, take what's coming to you first, and then you can complain. Obey continues, "I was the class prefect...I had to say 'Obey first' to help [the teacher], to assist him. 'Obey First' then abbreviated to 'Obey.' And so, through that one, when I come into the school, they say 'Obey,' so that's how...it became so popular."

After he left school, Obey started working as a clerk and played music at night. In Lagos, as a member of the Fatayi Rolling Dollar highlife band, he started out as a conga player and worked his way up to lead guitar. In 1964, with support from West African Decca Records and inspiration from I.K. Dairo, he formed his own juju band called the International Brothers. They quickly had a hit single called "Ewa Wowun Ojumi Ri," or "People Come and See What I See." He remained with West African Decca and became its director, with more than 100 of his own albums, most of which went gold. Obey was one of the richest men in Lagos.

During the 70s, Obey became more and more religious, and he changed the name of his band to the Inter-Reformers. By 1982, he was confessing his sins publicly on his record jackets. "There are many things I have done in the past which I now regret and will never dare to repeat," he said on one. Later, he added, "As an artist you're exposed to a lot of things. A lot of temptation....Girls are always a problem." (He has a number of children but refuses to say just how many.) He has turned his nightclub into a church and plays juju for services there. "I use this media to preach Christ, to teach of Christ, which is a way of teaching people of the way of the Lord." But first and foremost, Chief Commander Obey is known for picking up where I.K. Dairo left off in developing juju. Obey continues the formation of his personal style—or "system" as it is referred to in Lagos—called "miliki," which means enjoyment, and he has added instruments over the years. However, the form of his juju remains classic.

Sunny Adé's experimentation, on the other hand, has covered a much wider range and has brought juju to its peak. His real name is Chief Sunday Adeniyi, and he was actually born a prince in the royal family of Ondo in 1947. His father, a missionary in the African church, died when Adé was eight. His mother had high hopes that Adé would become a lawyer, so he kept it secret from her when he began playing with the highlife band of Moses Olaiya in Lagos. His cover was finally blown when friends of the family saw the band on a tour of Ondo. He avoided his mother's disapproval and disappointment by telling her that he was only playing music to work his way through school.

While Adé played conga with the band, he gradually learned guitar. Then, when Moses Olaiya left the band to go into government, Adé was able to take over as leader. He changed the name to Sunny Adé and His Green Spot Band, and sales went from twenty-three copies for their first single, to 500,000 for the second (the one that praised the soccer team). With such a smash behind him, Adé probably could have just ridden this success and continued making hits. But Adé is relentless in his quest to remain innovative and to improve his skill on guitar. Besides introducing new instruments into the music, in 1971 he made the first non-stop dancing albums; since then, his Nigerian releases use a complete side of a record for each song. Subsequently, he was also the first to get his performers to stand up and dance during their shows.

Musically, Adé has become an amazing guitarist and has done more than any other performer to create integrated textures out of the highly varied instrumental sounds produced by his large orchestra. In Adé's system, instruments in each range work together to develop special polyrhythms for that range. For example, shakers, cowbells, and the high guitar create one skein on top; bass and talking drums create another on bottom. The sounds are balanced so no one instrument outshines another, and the textures change from one section to another. Adé's fan club named his style "Synchro System" because of the manner in which all his instruments work together. Today, he tries to recreate this sound as accurately as possible on recordings.

Adé's musical accomplishments, coupled with his diplomatic

Jak Kilby

Chief Commander Ebenezer Obey leads the Inter-Reformers.

skills, have brought him honorable title after honorable title, beginning in 1974 when he was named "Master Guitarist." In 1976, Nigerian newspapers and magazines joined to choose a musician of the year. "After consulting the kings of different towns and the people teaching music in those towns," Adé told writer Bill Milkowski, "I was the musician of the year. And they made it so high—prestigious—to the extent that it's taller than a king. They put a crown on my head and gave me a traditional shoe, and ever since then I am King Sunny Adé. It is an honor like the ones they give to Elvis Presley." Later, the government named him "Minister of Enjoyment."

Both Adé and Obey profess to be uninterested in politics, believing more in "love." But both are active in PMAN, the Nigerian musicians' union, which has been attempting to get off the ground for many years. PMAN concerns itself mainly with trying to prevent record piracy (it is estimated that over fifty percent of the recordings sold in Nigeria are pirated), trying to increase the availability of instruments (which are either banned from importation or heavily taxed as luxury items), and, to some extent, helping the plight of the great majority of struggling musicians.

When asked why he does not produce more up-and-coming juju musicians himself, Ebenezer Obey replied, "It depends on the upcoming artist, if he likes to play like me or like Sunny or [if he wants] to try what I did, to get his own type of music. All that thing is not very easy. So that's why the young musicians have not been [very successful]. They try and play like me or like Sunny."

The only two juju artists who got their "own type of music" and were able to reach the base camp near the pinnacle where Obey and Adé sit are Admiral Dele Abiodun and Prince Segun Adewale. Both have been aggressively marketing fusions of juju, rock, and highlife. Abiodun is an unusual case—he is from Bendel state, not a Yoruba area. He was first attracted to music when he saw an article about the Young Pioneers School of Music, founded by Nkrumah in Ghana. Abiodun took the tuition money he had been given for secondary school and left for Ghana straightaway. He began playing bass in Accra highlife bands. Returning to Lagos, he formed a highlife band with another Nigerian. The friend eventually left music to become a church leader and, in 1969, Abiodun formed his own juju band called Sweet Abby and the Top Hitters Band. Obey and Adé were already firmly entrenched on their pinnacle, but Abiodun believed "I have some other new things to offer the public. I brought in my own...mixture of highlife, juju, and rock. That's why I call it adawa system, 'doing your own thing.'" Although acknowledging that his music is within the Sunny Adé school of juju guitar, Abiodun's style is different enough to have made a mark with his adawa Super Series of records. Whether or not he introduced the steel pedal guitar, he makes the most extensive use of it. His characteristic intros often use the slide sound continually for minutes on end, and his baselines sometimes bounce hopefully around country-and-western chord changes. His music also has a strong Afro-beat sound on occasion. Abiodun recently had some problems because of the proposed title of his latest album: *Confrontation*. After five months of delay, it now has a chance to be released under the title of *Oro Ayo*, which means "good tidings."

A brash challenger, Segun Adewale, has taken a much more aggressive stance with his Yoruba popular, or "yo-pop" music. He differentiates it from older juju because of its "kick and start" pacing: "Once I start I am right away in top gear....I think yo-pop has more chance in Europe than juju because the energy is more in tune with the European pace of life. They rush all the time," he says. Despite all his talk of fast tempos and fusions with funk, reggae, rock, and jazz, Adewale's music, as played with the Superstars International Band, sounds very much like juju. Though he's about eight years younger than Sunny Adé, Adewale obtained a solid grounding in classic juju by playing with the legendary I.K. Dairo. He first became famous when he shared top billing with another up-and-coming juju artist, Sir Shina Peters, in the Western Brothers band. When the duo split up in 1977 it was big news in

Segun, a member of Sunny Adé's tightly coordinated African Beats, at the Ritz in New York.

Claudia Thompson

Nigeria and set the stage for the 1980 creation of Adewale's own Superstars group. They introduced yo-pop with a song called "Endurance," which became a dancing favorite. Unlike many juju stars, Adewale has no qualms about singing in English, though from the awkward results (which can be heard on "Adewale Play For Me") perhaps he should. Otherwise, he's vitally innovative in the development of juju.

With all the competition between juju stars to add new sounds and instruments to their various "systems," one new branch of juju comes as a complete surprise, though it is consistent with the re-Africanization tendency of African popular music. *Fuji* music, which started to gain immense popularity in Lagos around 1980, is juju with nothing new added; on the contrary, all the instruments are dropped except for percussion. On top of this, a singer declaims incessantly in a Mediterranean singing style. Fuji is the new hot music of the Lagos underclasses. In beer parlors, at outdoor parties, and in the streets in front of record kiosks all over the city, people sway in a blissful trance, doing a characteristic dance: for instance, the men freeze the upper body and jerk hands, neck, or torso out at strange angles, while the feet keep up a shuffle; a change in drumming is a signal to lower the body to the ground. As in juju, fuji has two stars who absolutely dominate the field: Alhaji Chief Waseew Ayinde Barrister, who claims to have founded the form, and Alhaji Chief Ayinla Kollington, known as Baba Alatika. Both are very young and are religious Muslims, and Barrister has just been awarded a chieftancy title as the Bada Barawu of Ogijo.

Barrister's fuji—"talazo fuji,"—he says is "equivalent to the rock music which turns the youth on.... Very soon, I am going to take talazo across the frontiers of Nigeria and make Nigeria great." He also claims that his ultimate ambition is to become a barrister or lawyer, the source of his name. Kollington calls his brand "bata fuji" because he uses the double-headed ceremonial bata drums, over which he chants his signature pieces such as "Awa Na Re, ju bayi to awa tanse bembe le Eko ile," which means "here we are, we are not more than this, we who give joy to people." "You know, fuji is even faster than disco music.... That is the brand of music I am going to dish out this year. This is my year," he says of 1985.

Fuji's biggest year yet was actually election year, 1983, when both Barrister and Kollington put out tracks to inspire all the candidates to "unite Nigeria for posterity." The side-long cuts discuss all of recent Nigerian history, with prayers and wishes interjected. Barrister's version is backed with a tribute to Bobby Benson, who died that year. To lyrics such as "It is the same death that strikes at the master swimmer and the ace hunter," Barrister adds the horn riffs of Benson's famous "Taxi Driver" song, while his thirty-five-man percussion ensemble creates layer upon layer of traditional rhythms. In fact, everything can be thrown into fuji. Praises are popular, along with moral lessons, gossip, and descriptions of a recent tour. The language, as in juju, is Yoruba, with English popping in here and there.

With sales in the hundreds of thousands for such traditional-style music, it is obvious that juju musicians have no need to worry about which way the fad winds blow in the West, or whether one of them will be named the next Bob Marley. They maintain a vital role in a still strong culture.

D I S C O G R A P H Y

Sunny Adé	JUJU MUSIC	Mango 9712, or Island ILPS 9712
Sunny Adé	SYNCRO SYSTEM	Mango 9737, or Island ILPS 9737
Sunny Adé	BOBBY	Sunny Adé Records 36
Traditional Artists	DRUMS OF THE YORUBA	Ethnic Folkways FE 4441
Ebenezer Obey	SOLUTION	Sterns 1005
Ebenezer Obey	SINGING FOR THE PEOPLE	Afrodisia DWAPS 578
Ebenezer Obey	MILIKI PLUS	Virgin VM7
I.K. Dairo	I.K. DAIRO	Afrodisia DWAPS 2184
Dele Abiodun	TOP HITTERS BAND	Olumo Records ORPS 79
Segun Adewale	PLAY FOR ME	Rounder Records 1003
Ayinla Kollington	NIGERIAN ELECTION	Kollington Rec. KRLPS 3

Emanuel Bovet

SENEGAL

GUINEA-BISSAU

Dakar

Bissau

Conakry

GUINEA

SIERRA LEONE

Monrovia

LIBERIA

UPPER VOLTA

MALI

Ouagadougou

IVORY COAST

Abidjan

GRIOTS

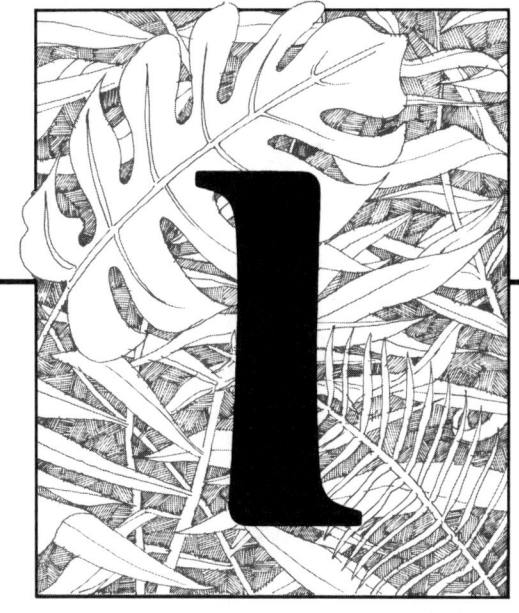

In a small village of the Sahel, it is said, a young girl named Bintou was well known for her beauty. Her father, a cotton trader, needed a favor from the president of the large trading city on the coast. When the favor was granted, the father gave Bintou to the president in appreciation. Bintou was brought to the president's magnificent palace in the sparkling new capital, sixty miles from the noisy, sprawling port city that used to be the national seat.

In the city there were boulevards a quarter of a mile wide, empty except for the Mercedeses of the rich and the motorcades of dignitaries. Bintou had her own house on the palace grounds, resplendent with Persian carpets and golden water faucets, but she was lonely. She was only twenty-five and the president was eighty, and Bintou could tell that the president's wife was very jealous of her. There were few other people around, and no one who could speak her native language, Mandingo.

So Bintou sent for a griot—a member of the ancient family of musicians that had the ancestral right to serenade the kings of the Empire of Mali—from her home region. Fode Kouyate, a young griot with a powerful voice and physique, had begun learning the ancient instruments and songs when he began to talk. He was willing to leave the poverty of his village and come to the coast capital, where Bintou bought him a fine house and a car. Hour after hour, he would sing to her of her native land, accompanying himself on guitar and kora, the twenty-one-string harp that is the griot's traditional instrument. He sang of her beauty and of his feelings toward her, for the two had become very close. Suddenly, at the age of twenty-seven, Bintou died. No one knew what caused his death, but people spoke

Mory Kante in his Paris apartment with a griot's garb and kora.

in hushed tones about a curse of jealousy from the president's wife.

Fode Kouyate fell into depression and poverty. He lost his house and his car and was set adrift in Treichville, the slum of the coast city. Hearing of his plight, a well-established distant relative decided to help Fode Kouyate by producing a record with him. Fode Kouyate went to Paris for the studio sessions. He was shown how to use an electric guitar and his songs were arranged for a large group that included a piano, bass guitar, synthesizers, trumpets, saxophones, a drum set, congas, and a chorus of two French women who sounded like munchkins. On top of all this, the griot's startling voice, with all its emotion, was heard singing, "Bintou is gone, but Bintou will always be here because I sing this song."

When Fode Kouyate came back to Treichville, his song was heard playing in all the record kiosks and maquis. Cassettes had sold by the hundreds of thousands, but unfortunately they were all pirate copies. Fode received no money and established no career from the album, so he disappeared into the street world of the coast city, occasionally playing in bars and maquis in exchange for beers and small change.

A search for Fode through the dark streets of Treichville brings only false leads and laughter from the bar owners and prostitutes. Finally, one points to an alleyway where there is a maquis in which a griot plays every night. It turns out the maquis is itself an alleyway between two low concrete-block buildings. The extension of the tin roof of one of the buildings provides shelter, and a makeshift gate closes it off from the street. Inside the gate, a young man of powerful build plays a guitar as if it were a kora, tripping down quick pentatonic runs with two fingers. A much younger guitarist plays rolling arpeggios in accompaniment. The griot is singing in Mandingo. A new, familiar face enters the maquis and the griot sings of this person's family line. The honored one gives him a few francs or buys him a Fanta because he doesn't drink beer.

The maquis is packed with people whose attention level ranges from totally unaware of the music to completely mesmerized. At one table, a large fat woman is teased seductively by two friends; she rolls across their laps, and her chair falls backwards with a crash. An abusive drunk goes into the toilet cabinet and someone locks him in; everyone in the maquis laughs hysterically. Two men begin to fight, and the griot's song admonishes them to stop. Between verses, the griot replies to the listeners' comments about his song, keeping up a running dialogue. Rain begins to fall in torrents; plastic plates float out into the street. Finally, the single bare bulb in the maquis fizzles and goes out. But the griot continues to play, now mixing rock 'n' roll strumming with his modal runs, singing about

Lauren Deutsch

The tools of a modern griot; clockwise from bottom left: guitar, balafon, dundungo, tamo (small talking drum), dousongoni, voice, kora, sabaro, junkuran, kalimba (hand piano), kutiro, and shekere.

a girl named Suzy. He breaks a string and stops playing. In the dark, he says he is not Fode Kouyate, though he knows of him. His name, the griot says, is Mahama. He comes from Guinea, and he came to the city to find work, but he hasn't found any yet. He plays in the maquis every night except Sunday.

In somewhat more luxurious surroundings, a restaurant near Les Halles in Paris called le Kinkeliba, another griot praises the clothing and hairstyles of the diners while playing a kora. In contrast to the griot in Treichville who wore a t-shirt and jeans, this man is dressed in flowing white robes. Sourakata Kouyate says he was born into a family of griots in Tambacounda, East Senegal, in 1955. "It is only those of the Kouyate family who are griots and have the right and obligation to play kora," he says. From a very early age he was given lessons on this instrument, which has a large calabash and cowskin resonator and a redwood neck. His father also taught him balaphon (the African wooden xylophone) and kone, a small guitar-like instrument. He is familiar with the detailed lineage of the great Mandingo families, from Soundiata Keita in the Middle Ages to Almamy Samory Toure of the recent past.

Ancient songs, such as "Djanjon," recounting the coming of age of a young emperor in the era of Soundiata, are the first songs learned by young griots. Traditionally, the young griot also develops his memory skills so he can begin to acquire the immense amount of knowledge and oration that is the basis of Mandingo culture. (When he is older he will be known as the "bag of words," the phrase used to describe an old and very knowledgeable griot.) With this abundance of information, he can sing and please the local nobles, at whose beck-and-call the griot remains. This makes the griot class an inferior one. They are not supposed to work for themselves but must depend on the patronage of the nobles. But at the same time, the griots, like the praise singers in Nigeria, are feared. Their words have power, both in themselves and in the fact that they may be heard far and wide.

According to Sourakata, the Emperor Soundiata gave the name Kouyate to one of his griots, and it means "you can get everything you need at home." He also recounts that the first kora was built by Manyan Kouyate and had only three strings. A later king requested one with a string for every day of the week. Finally, King Kelefa asked for an instrument that could play a song for the whole people; his griot built the twenty-one-string kora because Kelefa had twenty-one wives.

A Westerner, hearing the kora for the first time, might be amazed at how similar the instrument sounds to a country blues guitar. Of course, the music is not organized in twelve-bar patterns of chord changes; there's only one base string per mode, and each string plays only one note since the kora is basically a harp. But you can definitely hear the origins of the blues there. Often, in traditional situations, a griot will be accompanied by a second kora player. This accompanist does not sing, but plays repetitive patterns, from which the first griot departs with high, quick-descending ornamental runs that are similar to the Arabic-sounding vocal lines he sings. For dancing celebrations a griot may be accompanied by an ensemble of seven or eight drums.

The griot, as a professional musician who praises and tells stories, exists in many parts of Africa, but in the inland areas of West Africa (once dominated by the empires of Mali and Islam) the strong caste system gives the Mandingo griot his birthright. This area includes Mali, Guinea, Senegal, Burkina Faso (Upper Volta), the Ivory Coast, and parts of neighboring countries as well. Since all of these countries were colonized by France, many griots wind up in Abidjan, the show-biz capital of francophone Africa, or in Paris.

Specific histories vary with each griot. Sourakata Kouyate was taken out of his traditional milieu by a restauranteur who, in 1977, brought him to Dakar and then to Paris. Besides his job in the restaurant, he also plays with a group called "les Lezards," made up of koras, guitars, kone (a small African guitar), and a singer who chants in Bambara. Lamine Konte, son of the famous Casamance (a region of Senegal) griot Dialy Keba Konte (known throughout Africa as "Le Vieux") played in theatrical productions in Dakar and came to France for the first time to participate in arts festivals. In 1971, he established residence in France, and since then has been recording albums of traditional kora music and collaborating with Western musicians, most notably in the 1979 Senegalese film *Bako,* and also with Stevie Wonder for the film *The Secret Life of Plants.* Foday Musa Suso, a Mandingo griot from Gambia, came to the United States via the Institute of African Studies at the University of Ghana. In the U.S., he formed a band called Mandingo Griot Society, which mixes West African music with folk rock, and adds a splash of East Indian music here and there. But of all the emigre griots, it's probably Mory Kante, "the Mandingo Lion," who puts on the best show—like the 1983 one that ran in the Hotel Ivoire in Abidjan. The first half was set in a village, and a griot ensemble with drums played while Mory Kante sang. Then Mory came out of a puff of smoke, wearing a shimmering pink suit, playing an electric kora, and backed by a full electric ensemble. He drove the entire audience onto the dance floor.

In the 60s and early 70s, local dance bands played Congolese music and the usual dance-hall mix of the other foreign musics— Cuban, soul, and later reggae—in the urban dance halls of the griot-rich areas. However, in the late 70s, the thirst for popular music in local languages grew, especially in the capital cities of Dakar, Senegal, and Bamako, Mali. In Dakar, this trend was encouraged by the nationalist philosophy of president and poet Leopold Senghor; in

Youssou N'Dour, with Super Etoile de Dakar, sings it in Wolof.

Bamako, by a biennial contest for the best songs from the best pop groups of each region, which exists to this day.

It is not always the griots who lead these local dance bands. In fact, the biggest band in Mali is led by someone who is from a caste that is forbidden to play music. Salif Keita, whose group is Les Ambassadeurs, is from the royal class. "It is the musicians who are supposed to play for us!" his angry parents told him, "not the other way around." Salif Keita was born in Djoliba, a small village about thirty-five miles from Bamako. His ambition was to be a teacher, and he went to school in Bamako for that purpose, but he failed and wound up with nothing to do. "I decided to go into music because it is a better way to teach than even working in a classroom, and you reach many more people." He began singing in a small club or "grain" in one of Bamako's poor, and overcrowded areas. He sings in

Mandingo, and his voice has the power and ability to consistently reach strange, piercingly high tones, but it can also be filled out with soft tones that give it extra poignancy. In 1972, Salif Keita was discovered by the saxophonist Tidiani Kone who led the orchestra of the Buffet Hotel. During the three months that he played with this band, Keita became famous throughout Mali. Eventually, however, he had an argument with the orchestra's leader and was kicked out of the band during a tour in western Mali.

When he came back to Bamako, Keita found work with the resident band of a club called the Motel. The group was called les Ambassadeurs du Motel. At the time (1975), the band was doing the usual mixture of Congolese and Cuban music. But Keita met a guitarist named Kante Manfila at the Motel, and together they began to change things. Manfila, a much older man, had been known for decades as master of the *guitare sèche* ("dry guitar"), the African name for acoustic guitar. He was famous for using folk material adapted to the instrument. Keita and Manfila introduced this local music into the repertoire of les Ambassadeurs and added local rhythms to the backups so they were adapted to Keita's Mandingo vocals. Les Ambassadeurs became famous and, in 1977, Keita was honored with the title of Officer of the National Order by President Sekou Toure. Moved, Keita wrote a paean to African nationalism, "Manjou," a homage to the Guinean leader and a recounting of the history of the empires of Mali. It became a huge hit, and is still considered the most beautiful of les Ambassadeurs' work. More hits followed in quick succession: "Prinpin," which counsels youth to seek self-realization but avoid drugs and alcohol, and praises officials who are trying to fight drug and alcohol abuse; "Sidiki Bathily," which encourages continued faith in God despite bad luck; "Jean ou Paul," and a few others.

With the political turmoil in Mali in 1978, when a "gang of four" top officials were arrested for high treason, les Ambassadeurs found it opportune to leave Mali for Abidjan and try to go international. There, they became les Ambassadeurs Internationaux and found what all musicians look for—a producer. The producer, a Malian named Sako, took them to the United States to record two albums. He even gave them a contract in which seventy percent of the royalties went to the group. Unfortunately, the master tapes were somehow stolen and copied, without anyone's knowledge. Soon, there were thousands upon thousands of pirated copies of the albums on the African market, even before the release of the record. Accusations flew between the members of the group. Keita and Manfila, between whom there had always been slight tension and jealousy, grew antagonistic towards one another and finally split.

Salif Keita left the group and eventually created les Super Ambassadeurs, who have had a rocky time. Keita himself now spends part of his time in Mali, where he plays at the Motel, but is uncomfortable because of the rift he feels with his parents and with Paris, where he lives in a misbegotten high-rise in the ticky-tacky suburbs. An albino with reddish hair and small eyes, Keita has a strange presence, but exudes sincerity when he speaks of his family problems, his search for a producer, and his wariness of high technology. However, he is working to develop some very strong blends of high-tech funk and traditional music, which he hopes to release sometime in 1985.

Dakar, too, has recently been weaning itself from foreign music, and local rhythms have been gaining popularity there. The product of a long line of traditional musicians, Youssou N'Dour began his public career at age thirteen, singing as "Le Petit Prince de Dakar." In 1977, he formed his own group, le Super Étoile de Dakar, with lyrics in Wolof (a Senegalese language) and talking drums. The result was a sort of Wolof funk that had young people dancing traditional dances in the Dakar dance halls, and gave N'Dour a string of hit albums and several tours to Europe. N'Dour's success has encouraged other bands to look towards their roots for inspiration. Traditions are not hard to find in a city that hosts the *lamb*, a sort of wrestling ceremony performed to the accompaniment of griots and drummers and that is a favorite entertainment in the popular quarters, such as Fass Paillote.

One group that has felt the call to go local is Xalam, who has been around since the late 60s, doing soul imitations in the Dakar dance halls. At the end of the 70s, the band took a sabbatical from playing, locked themselves up in their shared house, and worked up a fusion between Senegalese music and jazz-rock. The Senegalese felt this mix was too folkloric, so Xalam took their music to Paris. And the Parisians love it, even though it does feel more like jazz (which, granted, contains a lot of African elements) than African popular music. Besides hit albums and tours, Xalam's rhythm section has worked with the Rolling Stones and recorded a soundtrack for the African Pavilion at Disneyworld.

The group to make the biggest splash recently, both in Senegal and abroad, has been Toure Kunda. They are three brothers who are not from the griot class. "We belong to a family which is from the artisan's caste," says the eldest, Ismail. "Our father was a shoemaker; he worked the skins of animals to make shoes and bags. The griots are the ones who are supposed to play music, while the nobles aren't allowed. But an artisan—a shoemaker, a weaver, an ironmonger, a jeweler—is much closer to the griot . . . they are also at the disposition of the nobles, because it's the noble class that's supposed to consume this sort of thing."

Like Kante, the three brothers come from the Casamance region, south of the wedge of a country called Gambia that divides Senegal in two and is in close proximity to many cultures. "In lower Casamance you find Peuls...the Baymanks...and the Douala, and the Mankagnes and the Mandingos who are in Gambia (which I con-

Pierre Akendengue: an African poet with a wide musical vocabulary.

Jak Kilby

sider part of Casamance) and Wolof," explains one of the brothers. "And we live eighteen kilometers from Guinea-Bissau, fifty kilometers from Gambia, and seventy kilometers from Guinea-Conakry." On top of this cultural mix, the brothers all have the same father but different mothers, and each mother speaks a different language. Finally, they had a Catholic music education and exposure to international music on the radio, to percussion instruments of the region, and to some guitar. All these things combined, they were in an ideal position to create a pan-African music.

Ismail went to Paris in 1975 to see what could be done in the music scene there. He sent for his brothers, Sixu and Amadou, a year later. They experimented first with reggae and general African music with mixed results. Then they got more excited about a specific rhythm that they had heard in a traditional ceremony in their area. "It's a sort of initiation rite which is called 'Djamba Dong,' which is the 'Dance of the Leaves,' a part of the festival," Ismail explains. Why the Dance of the Leaves? To assure sustenance to the initiates when they go into the holy forest to submit to their initiation into life, girls or boys from eight to fifteen years of age. They learn how to become a man or a woman, how to understand life, how to behave, how to have hope, etc. And during all these initiation rites, there is music all around—a lot of percussion."

In the beginning, Toure Kunda mostly used percussion and voices, with the balaphon and the kora. Then they began to add electric instruments to replace the traditional ones, something they feel they have the right to do. "As the eldest brother," asserts Ismail, "I'm thirty-five years old, and when I started making music the electric guitar and the electric piano already existed in my region. So there was no reason not to use them." In Paris, they taught French musicians to play guitar and synthesizer to simulate kora and balaphon, which is not just a matter of technique. "It was difficult for the guitarist to learn to play like a kora, but he had great interest in learning. Before doing a song, we explain in detail not only how to play the music, but its significance as well. We say, for example, this song speaks of peasants or of our parents. And it's in Mandingo and the Mandingos play like this and the guitar must sound like that. And [the guitarist] tries to do it afterwards, and so on. At our house we have a large collection of traditional music on record that they can listen to. And we find that we do honor to the tradition, and that what we do with the piano and guitar is to amplify the effect of the traditional instruments."

Their first album, *Toure Kunda*, was composed of gorgeous folk melodies and percussion over steady reggae, rock, or Arabic base rhythms. Its exposure helped them build momentum, and it got

Emanuel Bovet

Salif Keita feels that music is the best medium for teaching.

them a lot of club dates. Then, during a 1983 performance at the Chapel des Lombards in Paris, brother Amadou died suddenly, apparently from exhaustion. A younger brother, Ousmane, was drafted to replace him and revive the demoralized group. Their memorial album, *Amadou Tilo,* was a tour-de-force of rolling rhythms and modal melodies. They toured extensively in Europe and Algeria, preparing for their triumphal return to West Africa. For, despite their success elsewhere, it remained to be seen whether their fusions would be accepted in their native land. As they got closer to home, through Mali and the Ivory Coast, they were received with more and more enthusiasm. Finally, they were met in Demba

Diop by a cheering, dancing crowd, including the president of Senegal. Their acceptance in Senegal was confirmed.

Toure Kunda recorded an acoustic album of traditional songs before they went completely electronic in their latest album, *Natalia*, with the help of producer Bill Laswell of Material. Upon its release, they embarked on a tour of the United States, which they see as very important. "We think because of our origins we have ties with black Americans, by jazz, which existed from the memories of people who were taken from their land, by blues, and by the fact that all the music played by black Americans has affinities with ours. We have to make them discover it. For the moment they are too content with themselves, they have a lot to learn about the reality: the origins of their music in African music."

But do they still think they are speaking to Africans as traditional griots? "We are very involved. For instance, in the song 'Samara,' we speak for our parents, who in the past were peasants, to whom it was demanded that they pay taxes. And my ancestor says to them: 'How can you ask me to pay taxes if I don't have any money—I only have my fields. It doesn't go well even though I'm working hard. I refuse to pay you taxes.' And we've created a character through whom we tell this story of taxes. And our parents, when they heard the song, they said it was too daring, because they felt it was

Toure Kunda in New York City, left to right: Sixu, Ismail, and Ousmane Toure.

themselves about whom we were speaking."

This may well exemplify the role of the modern griot—to set people thinking about how things should be done in modern Africa, through tales of the past—for often it is dangerous to comment openly. In this role, Gabonian singer/poet Pierre Akendengue finds himself well within the tradition. "I situate myself in the griot tradition," he says, "even if this personage itself is rare in Nandipo, my native region, because I transmit orally the events of reality." Akendengue, who came to France in the mid-60s to study psychology and then stayed to develop his personal means of inter-African musical expression, uses a wide range of traditional and modern techniques. The reality he sings about encompasses a continent that has been cut into pieces, that is hardpressed by exploitation and rapid change, and whose citizens are searching for their individual and collective identity in the modern world. But even though this musical search may uncover a synthesizer playing the part of a balaphon and a double-necked electric guitar simulating a kora, it is still possible to imagine Fode Kouyate in all this, searching for his patroness Bintou, lost long ago but living in song.

D I S C O G R A P H Y

Fode Kouyate	HOMMAGE	Tek Records NS 6052
Foday Musa Suso	KORA MUSIC	Folkways FW 8510
Mandingo with Foday Musa Suso	WATTO SITTA	Celluloid 6103
Lamine Konte	BAKO L'AUTRE RIVE	Safari Ambiance 61002
Mory Kante	N'DIARABI	Mandingo Productions 000123
Les Ambassadeurs	DANCE MUSIC FROM WEST AFRICA	Rounder 5013
Youssou N'Dour	IMMIGRES	Celluloid 6709
Toure Kunda	LIVE PARIS-ZIGUINCHOR	Celluloid 6106
Toure Kunda	NATALIA	Celluloid 6113
Xalam	GOREE	Celluloid 6656
Pierre Akendengue	MANDO	CBS 25355

ZIMBABWE

Johannesburg

SOUTH
AFRICA

Jak Kilby

MBAQANGA

baqanga: as a trumpet prodigy hooked on bebop, Hugh Masekela wouldn't touch the stuff. According to one jazz-loving critic of the time, it was just pap that the record companies could unload on the rural and township consumer cheaply, "something to pat your foot to, anything with bounce or rhythm, original or copied, but it must sell." But now, after twenty years of self-imposed exile from South Africa, a country he won't return to until "it becomes a humane area," Masekela basks in the mbaqanga rhythms coming from a portable recording studio just over the South African border in Botswana. "Instead of having to teach the music, I'm reveling in it," he told writer Barney Hoskyns. "It's like a Brazilian will come to New York and teach a few guys like Ron Carter, and they'll play it right, but when he goes back and gets Sevrina de Olivera, he'll just swim in it."

Mbaqanga, the dance music of the black townships of South Africa, thrives despite the inhumanity of apartheid and the occasional disapproval of the music by sophisticated critics. The music has grown up in a country where blacks have little control over radio, recording, and concert production situations and where, for much of its history, mixed-race audiences and bands have either required special permits and segregated box offices or been illegal altogether. Regional black music has been both looked down upon by whites and berated by politically conscious blacks as a vehicle that furthers the government's attempt to develop a separate and non-threatening black culture. It's been a victim to both governmental restrictions and international anti-apartheid boycotts that isolate South Africa from the rest of the world.

The government's obsession with group separation, on the other

Hugh Masekela, a South African jazz trumpeter, embraces his roots.

hand, has helped to provide the most diverse influences possible for the music. For example, separate radio stations broadcast regional music for the major ethnic groups—Zulu, Xhosa, Northern Sotho, Southern Sotho, Tswana, Venda, and Tsonga. Other stations provide rock, classical, easy-listening, and jazz for whites. Afrikaners love country-and-western; young whites have kept up with the punk and new wave fads.

There is a richer mix of music in South Africa than exists in most areas of the world. And mbaqanga sounds quite different than the popular music of other parts of black Africa. It's a stomping, jarring music that often seems closer to Louisiana Zydeco blues or quick reggae than to, for instance, the polyrhythmic rhumba of countries a few hundred miles north.

The musical mix on the radio and on recordings, widely available in the townships since the 30s, accounts for part of this difference. But more important is the difference between the traditional music of Southern Africa and the traditional music of the rest of black Africa. Specifically, the south lacked the instrumental polyrhythms of the rest of the continent, for several reasons. First of all, there are few traditional instruments. The ones that do exist—single drums, rattles, clapping hands—keep a heavy, steady beat with lighter shuffles in between, while choral voices in open harmonies provide the rhythmic interest by staggering the cycles of their repetitions. It's been said that the lack of instruments was due in part to the lack of materials with which to make them on the largely treeless veld that covers most of the country. But it also seems that the stamping rhythm and light equipment are akin to the military nature of the Zulu clan that came to dominate the whole area in the nineteenth century. The Zulus were a small family group until the 1820s, when Chaka Zulu, a brilliant military strategist, burst out of the Natal area with his army and began a series of raiding campaigns. He eventually built a huge empire by devastating the other groups in the region. The result was a *mfecane*, or a scattering of peoples, reaching as far as into present-day Zimbabwe.

At around the same time, the Boers (descendants of Dutch settlers, now called Afrikaners) gave up struggling with the British for control of the Cape area and marched on the "Great Trek" into the interior of Africa, founding two republics, the Transvaal and the Orange Free State. The Boer republics were conquered by the British in two wars before South Africa became an independent country in 1910, but the extremely nationalistic Afrikaner party won control of the government in the (exclusively white) elections of 1948. It is that party that is the backbone of apartheid.

Both kinds of European descendants, the Boers and the Afrikaners, cooperated in the massive displacement of black peoples that began with the discovery of precious and semiprecious minerals in the late nineteenth century, most significantly the discovery of gold in the Johannesburg area in 1886. The government, in a series of repressive measures including land grants to whites and heavy tax levies on black farmers, forced hundreds of thousands of black male workers to go to Johannesburg to seek work in the mines. Living in townships, large conglomerations of workers' barracks on the out-skirts of the city, these men were separated from their families and the music of their home regions. They would gather in the shebeens or illegal drinking pubs, to drink *skokiaan*, a potent alcoholic beverage made from yeast fermented in water. In the shebeens, they would play music on whatever instruments were at hand—old guitars, pianos, concertinas, and homemade percussion. The result was something called *marabi* music.

The small class of educated blacks in the townships looked down on marabi, preferring more Westernized forms of entertainment such as a sort of ragtime with Zulu singing, or a European cabaret-style music. In the 20s, phonograph records began to be sold in large volumes in the townships. Record companies tried to sell the Latin-American sounds that took off like crazy in the rest of Africa, but the South Africans just were not interested. Their music had a much stronger affinity with jazz, which—especially in the swing and bebop eras—had a strong four-beat-to-the-bar feel. The big band music of Duke Ellington, Count Basie, and Louis Armstrong sparked numerous jazz bands in the townships around Johannes-burg: the Merry Blackbirds, the Harlem Swingsters, the Jazz Mani-acs, the Rhythm Clouds, and others. South African jazz had a marabi tinge to it, but the most popular bands—the Blackbirds and the Maniacs—had a purer swing sound and often played for white audiences. The Jazz Maniacs were organized by a former shebeen pianist, Solomon "Zulu Boy" Cele, who, according to journalists of the 40s, wanted to create a truly African big band idiom. However, Zulu Boy died in 1944, and the Maniacs added more swing numbers into their sets and remained popular well into the 50s. But, accord-ing to South African writer Muff Andersson, the Maniacs were very significant because "they carried the spirit of marabi through to the dance halls, and they provided inspiration for a new breed of jazzmongers—Dollar Brand, Hugh Masekela, Kippie Moeketsi, Jonas Gwangwa . . . and the like."

Masekela was born in 1939 in a township about 100 miles east of Johannesburg. He caught the jazz bug at the age of thirteen when he saw a film about trumpet player Bix Beiderbecke. Bishop Huddleston, an anti-apartheid community leader, helped Masekela

Anthony Howarth/Camera Press/Photo Trends

A houseboy plays pennywhistle against the brick wall of his white employer's home in Johannesburg.

get a trumpet and begin lessons with a member of the Native Johannesburg Municipal Band. Soon after that, Masekela joined a local jazz band called the Merrymakers of Springs and continued to perfect his trumpet technique, studying with the horn players in that band. Soon, Masekela was getting a lot of attention; Dizzy Gillespie even sent him records from the States. He listened to Clifford Brown, Gillespie, and Miles Davis, and by 1956, he was "playing nothing but bebop."

Meanwhile, as jazz was catching on, other types of township music were developing. The Zulu penchant for a big, open choral sound was being expressed in a style called *mbube*. It was one of the earliest types of township music to be recorded and, in the beginning, provided a style for Zulu language versions of American tunes. Mbube groups have as many as ten or twelve singers and, in the music's original form, use no instruments. The name "mbube" possibly comes from the Zulu word *imbube*, meaning lion; the most popular mbube song worldwide was "Wimoweh" ("The Lion Sleeps Tonight"), written by Solomon Linda and recorded by Miriam Makeba and a number of American groups in the early 60s. The voices in mbube make lush, uniform choral harmonies, all singing together in short phrases. Then they may break up into rhythm and melody sections or overlapping call-and-response, with a prominent deep bass voice. The sound may be organized without chord progressions, or it may verge on a gospel style. A few groups even have lyrics on Christianity, while others discuss rural problems. The most popular mbube group today is Ladysmith Black Mambazo, made up of members of Zulu-speaking families from Swaziland.

From mbube other forms of choral singing developed. Female groups, such as the Mahotella Queens, perform with backing bands and often sing call-and-response with a "groaner," a male vocalist with a raspy bass voice who keeps up a running exchange with the group and also comments about topical themes. On one Mahotella album, for example, the women sing about Marks, their guitarist and groaner, saying he's a wizard. He replies, "Listen to what my guitar can say, it says: awa awa, . . ." The king of the groaners was Simon Nkabinde. In the early 60s, schools would empty for miles around when he gave a stadium concert, as people streamed in to hear him gossip and brag. Touring all over the country, he proudly boasted that he was "The First Groaner to Fly."

Much of the township music today, especially the choral styles, is criticized for being politically naive and, in a sense, reactionary, because in singing of country life it panders to the government's goals of group segregation. But there's also a long-running tradition of freedom and protest singing. Many of these a cappella chants are based on slogans that relate to historic protests. "Azikwelwa" or "We refuse to ride," originated during a bus boycott after a fare-hike in 1943, but has been used during all boycotts since then. There are chants based on the slogans "Free Mandela," "Maatla ke a rona" (Power to the People), and many chants from the 50s recalling the women's protests against the passes required to enter white areas.

However, mbaqanga music developed primarily as a form of entertainment. It came out of the marabi of the shebeens, as well as the guitar accompaniment of traditional songs, with its highly repetitive lines overlapping in a call-and-response with the vocals. With the influence of jazz, all this music became known as jive or mbaqanga, which refers to a quickly made mealie bread and possibly, "quick money." In the 30s, when mbaqanga first started to get a lot of airplay, the slapdash fusions of African and Western material were looked down upon by anyone with a pretense of taste.

In the 40s, however, a style called *kwela* developed; it was a captivating street music that began to win over the harsh critics of jive. Kwela was first played by boys from the township of Alexandra outside of Johannesburg, who used pennywhistles and homemade guitars to simulate a mix of marabi and jazz. The name comes from the term used to describe the police vans that cruised the township streets to arrest illegal gamblers. One ruse used by the street-corner gamblers was to quickly hide everything related to gambling when the police vans approached, and the gamblers would pretend they were gathered to listen to a young pennywhistler who would play until the police were gone. Lemmy "Special" Mabaso, the most famous pennywhistler, was under ten when a promoter discovered him playing in the streets of Alexandra.

During the 50s, a number of variety shows were put together by white promoters such as Ian Bernhardt in Johannesburg. They mixed kwela, jazz, and township jazz. The "Township Jazz" and "African Jazz and Variety" shows played to both black and white audiences and included all the performers who would become famous in the townships and beyond, including Lemmy "Special," Masekela, and Makeba. The creative center of these risky mixed-race ventures was Dorkay House in the center of Johannesburg, with rehearsal rooms for both theater and music and meeting space for a fledgling, much-needed musician's union and the African Music and Drama Association. The variety shows of the 50s culminated in a Broadway-style musical about a South African boxing champion named "King Kong." The show gave international exposure to Masekela and Kippie Moeketsi, who were in the orchestra, and Miriam Makeba, who was in the chorus. "King Kong" toured all of South Africa before moving to England for a highly successful year-long run, though the show was criticized for its lack of political content. The whole 50s era of variety shows and musicals is criticized by performers who, in retrospect, feel they were being exploited by the white promoters. They were paid extremely low wages despite the hint of glamor in the entertainment field. In addition, they were cheated into selling, for pennies, recording rights that made tens of thousands of pounds for the white-run recording companies.

Juliet Highet

Miriam Makeba tours around the world, singing South African song in a jazz-folk style.

This highly creative—if also highly exploitive—era came to an end as the repressive apartheid system became more severe. After the Sharpeville massacre of 1961, all gatherings of more than ten black people were prohibited for a while. At that time, Masekela was playing with Dollar Brand in a popular group called the Jazz Epistles. The group fell apart with the implementation of the harsh laws, and Masekela felt it was time to leave the country. At that point, Harry Belafonte, who had heard Miriam Makeba sing in London and was inspired to help her and other talented South African musicians, aided Masekela's emigration and he wound up at the Manhattan School of Music in New York. Belafonte, Makeba, and Dizzy Gillespie helped him establish a solid niche in the American jazz world. He climbed the pop charts in 1967 with "Up, Up, and Away" and "Grazin' in the Grass." "Grazin' " (times being what they were) became associated with marijuana, though it was actually based on a piece of Zambian music. In general, the African material in Masekela's work stayed on a light level, even though he formed groups with other South African emigres. He even went to London to record "*Home Is Where the Music Is*" album specifically with other African musicians. There, he found that these musicians "were out of touch with the African feel," as his producer Stewart Levine put it to *New Musical Express.* "The drummer played like he was in a polka band, and the thing turned back into a jazz album." The experience sparked off Masekela's quest to reinvigorate his roots. He went to West and Central Africa, winding up in Ghana with Fela Anikulapo Kuti, where he recorded two albums with the Hedzolleh Soundz highlife band.

But, meanwhile, mbaqanga was coming into its own in South Africa, elevated from slapdash "radio music" by a number of innovators. In 1964, a group called the Malombo Jazz Men astonished a crowd of 40,000 gathered at Orlando Stadium in Soweto for the Castle Lager Jazz Festival. Each jazz group in the competition was supposed to play their own version of the jazz standard "Bag's Groove." Malombo opened up with a bluesy mixture of Pedi and Venda rhythms, tonal tom-tom playing, and flute-playing inspired by penny whistles and American jazz flute player Roland Kirk. They won first prize and went on to record and develop their music and tour around the world during the next twenty years. The core of the group is Philip Tabane, a multi-instrumental virtuoso who has been known to play six flutes at the same time, multiple penny whistles while humming, and a guitar with his toes and teeth. Two other members of Malombo, Julian Bahula and Abe Cindi, went on to establish Jabula (based in London) and the Malopoets, respectively, but Tabane has stuck to his own peculiar vision to the present day. From 1965 to 1977, he toured the world with a nephew who he'd taught to play the traditional drums made of baobab roots and wild cowhide, an important part of Malombo's sound. But then the nephew disappeared during a tour to London in 1977. Tabane re-formed the group with three more young musicians, and they continue touring today, though he now finds that they have a growing audience among black South Africans as traditional rhythms in concert situations are more appreciated.

This trend is evident in the reception of pop-oriented material as well. The soul phenomenon was stronger in South Africa than anywhere else in Africa in the late 60s. Full-fledged soul groups, such as the Movers, filled up halls and stadiums with a Booker T. and the MGs-sound in its classic format—two guitars, an organ, and drums. Soul dances, such as the Monkey Jive, became all the rage, and groups often included two or three acrobatic dancers who did freezes and limb isolations that foreshadowed breakdancing. But then, in the 70s, soul groups started playing a punched up form of mbaqanga music, and the response was enormous. The Beaters, for example, had a soul repertoire until they put out the mbaqanga-influenced song "Harare." It was such a huge hit that they changed the group's name to Harare and continued exclusively with the mbaqanga mixtures. The Soul Brothers—who all developed a love of mbaqanga while growing up and working together in a textile

Philip Tabane, the core of Malombo, plays several flutes at once.

Thomas Mapfumo spreads the liberation message through his chimurenga music.

factory in Hammarsdale, Natal—went through the same process and wound up with a style that includes much more mbaqanga than rock. They are the first group to have sold mbaqanga records in the millions of copies.

The ever-widening appeal of mbaqanga, along with the steady appeal of rock in South Africa, has encouraged a new genre of crossover music that has gotten multiracial crowds together despite the continual roadblocks put up by apartheid. Juluka is the most successful of these bands, fronted by a pair of South Africans—one white and one black—that symbolizes a new hope for the forcibly divided nation. Johnny Clegg was born in the United Kingdom, then lived in Zimbabwe until the age of seven, when his family moved to Johannesburg. He learned Zulu guitar style as a teenager and began playing in the streets, where he hooked up with another street musician, Sipho Mchunu, a migrant worker from KwaZulu. The two began jamming together, and Sipho taught Johnny to dance. Juluka means "sweat" in Zulu, and much of the material of the music is based on Sipho's experience as a migrant worker, with the music a hearty blend of Zulu chants, mbaqanga, and early 70s rock 'n' roll, though the albums released by Warner Brothers stress the rock side. In performance, Clegg often competes with another black dancer in a form of dance contest used in rites of passage by the Zulus. Apparently, he is more than able to hold his own.

It was into this rich musical mix that Masekela, who sealed a contract with Jive Arista in early 1984, convinced Jive to ship a mobile twenty-four-track recording studio to Botswana. Parking near an inn ten miles outside the town of Gaborone, Masekela and his producer, longtime friend Stewart Levine, felt they had found a sonic heaven. There was silence all around except for an occasional bird chirp; they had some of the most modern recording equipment available; and, best of all, they had the musicians of Johannesburg only four hours away. Members of the Soul Brothers and Mandisa (who had provided vocals for Malcolm McLaren's "Duck Rock") were brought over from the city; Nigerian percussionist Gaspar Lawal was brought from London, along with a Fairlight synthesizer for sampling (digital recordings). The result, *Don't Go Lose It Baby*, is not exactly mbaqanga, but as Levine says, "We're too old to make esoteric music! . . . If this one happens, maybe it will open the doors for more South African music." Actually, the flip side of the album— what Masekela and Levine call the "south side"—does contain some generalized Afro-disco, and side one has a medley of "South Africa's Greatest Hits," with choral parts midway between Zulu and gospel. But more importantly, the title cut from the album reached number two on the U.S. dance charts, which encouraged Jive to contract Masekela to record albums of some of the mbaqanga groups, such as the Soul Brothers. Now Masekela will keep that trailer parked in Botswana, a conduit of South African music to the rest of the world.

If mbaqanga music has grown up along with the white-dominated regime in South Africa, the urban dance music of another country in southern Africa, Zimbabwe, was concocted especially to get rid of white minority control. *Chimurenga* music means "music of the struggle." It came out of the traditional music of the Shona people, who make up three quarters of the country's population. This ethnic homogeneity is somewhat unusual for a country whose borders were created by colonial interests. The borders almost make

The Mhuri Yehua Rwizi Mbira ensemble from Zimbabwe.

ethnic sense. The strongest characteristic of Shona music is the sound of the mbira, the local version of the hand piano. As a result, the electric guitars in chimurenga music imitate the fast-plinking patterns of this instrument. Of course, Zairian guitar styles were also partly inspired by hand-piano music, and so chimurenga music is similar to the Congolese music. Also as in Congolese music, the harmonies are filled out by horn lines and the dance momentum is effected by a quasi-rhumba bass. But the guitars are even faster and more twangy than in Zaire; and most importantly, the language is Shona, which almost everyone in Zimbabwe can understand, with the significant exclusion of the white settlers.

Before the 70s, the popular music of what was then Rhodesia was all foreign: Anglo-American rock, Congolese rhumba, and South African jive. Then, in 1973, a young musician named Thomas Mapfumo formed the Hallelujah Chicken Run Band, an ensemble that played traditional Shona music with electric instruments. The metaphorical meaning of traditional songs, such as "Shumba" (lion), were easily tied in with the aims of the two national liberation movements: ZANU, led by Robert Mugabe, and ZAPU, led by Joshua Nkomo. "Shumba," for example, speaks of the dangers of venturing too deeply into the jungle and could be taken as either a notification that the black guerrillas were in control of the interior or as a warning to watch out for the Rhodesian military. Chimurenga music and its politics were established.

In 1976, Mapfumo joined the Acid Band and began to write more overtly political songs. His hit of 1977, "Hokoyo!" ("Watch Out!") was banned from the national radio station and Mapfumo was jailed for a while. But this song, along with other chimurenga music, continued to be played on the "Voice of Zimbabwe," which broadcast from Maputo in Mozambique.

When Zimbabwe finally achieved independence on April 18, 1980, there was a musical celebration that not only included a Bob Marley concert in the national stadium, but led to the blossoming of other chimurenga bands. The Four Brothers, Elijah Madzikatire, and the Devera Mgwena Jazz Band, were now free to play whatever music they wanted. Dozens of hits celebrated independence. Now, in Harare, the capital city, the music is settling down as the urban good-time music, for its political mission is accomplished and, in the words of Mapfumo: "The sun has risen forever. There will never be darkness again in Zimbabwe." Hopefully, the mbaqanga bass lines will soon be allowed to roam South Africa as freely as the jangling guitars of chimurenga roam Zimbabwe.

D I S C O G R A P H Y

Various Artists	ZULU JIVE	Earthworks 2002
Various Artists	RHYTHM OF RESISTANCE	Shanachie 4308, or Virgin OVED 58
Various Artists	SOWETO	Rough Trade 37, or Zensor 05
Ladysmith Black Mambazo	INDUKU ZETHLI	Earthworks 2006
Malopoets	MALOPOETS	EMI 2402931
Hugh Masekela	TECHNO-BUSH	Jive/Arista HIP 11
Traditional Artists	SHONA MBIRA MUSIC	Nonesuch H-72077
Thomas Mapfumo	THE CHIMURENGA SINGLES: 1976–1980	Earthworks 2004
Various Artists	VIVA ZIMBABWE	Earthworks 2001

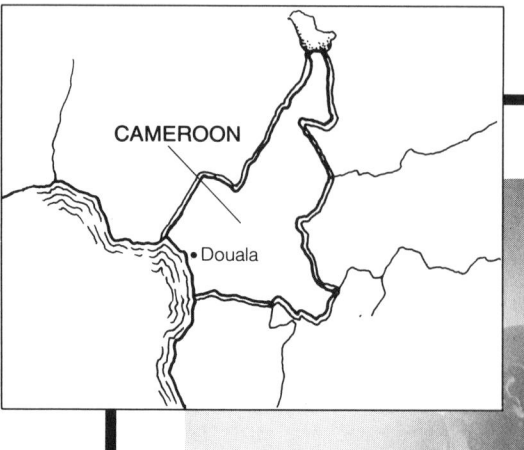

CAMEROON

• Douala

Jak Kilby

MAKOSSA

I n the 1980s, the *makossa,* the most popular dance rhythm among the people of Cameroon, has finally come into its own on the African charts. Sam Fan Thomas' souped-up makassi blend can be heard from the thousands of street speakers as often as the music of any Congolese artist; his *African Typic Collection* set new sales records. Moni Bile has made gold records every year recently. These two Cameroonians together sold more records in 1984 than any other African.

But Cameroonian musicans have been important in the international development of the new African popular music since its beginnings. For some unexplainable reason, in the post-World War II years, the port city of Douala was filled with musicians, both students who had left school and village musicians who were attracted to the city. At that time, neighboring Spanish (Equatorial) Guinea had an entertainment center in the city of Santa Isabel (now Malabo) on the island of Bioko (Fernando Po), which was a Havana-like haven for European tourists, full of hotel bars and fancy nightclubs. Many of the musicians of Douala went there to find work. They played the music that was the international rage then, the Latin rhythms of cha cha, rhumba, mambo, and samba. Some of the top Cameroonian musicians who'd worked in Santa Isabel came back to Douala to form the UV Coat Jazz Band, whose music already hinted at makossa rhythms. But other Cameroonians became the errant professional musicians of Africa, ready to go wherever the action was at the moment.

Manu Dibango must be ranked most adventurous in this set of musical voyagers, and one of the first to be completely at home in any modern musical genre and recording situation. He was born in

Manu Dibango, the creator of ''Soul Makossa'' and a professional world musician.

1934, in Douala. "We had all sorts of music at home—all the Afro-American things like tango, cha cha...and French singers...and the Cubans with sweet voices and a lot of percussion. My mother conducted the church choir—my family is Protestant—and we learned some music on the violin. This was during the war. If you tell people that you're African and you've learned music on the violin, they won't believe you. But that's how it is. Though at the same time there were those in the village who learned to play on the kora." Besides the violin Dibango began with a homemade flute and a handmade guitar, and occasionally snuck into his big brother's room to play on the real guitar his brother was allowed to bring home during school vacations.

When he was fifteen, Dibango was sent to France to study. "It was something like philosophy, or to become a doctor or a lawyer or something like that....I don't know, I never finished," he says with a deep laugh that sounds like the lyrics on all his recordings. "But I was sent there to study seriously, not to play music." His family's disapproval of music as a profession was very strong. Protestants in Cameroon, Dibango says, are very hardworking and never laugh. "Next door, there was a Catholic family, and even if the father was very religious, they could play drums at night. At our house, we didn't have the right." But he was allowed to take lessons in classical piano, since classical music study was considered part of a well-rounded education.

"Then on holiday in 1954, a friend lent me his saxophone and told me, 'since you have nothing to do, trying playing this.' So I took the saxophone, without knowing that maybe something was going to happen with this thing." Manu became hooked on it, took lessons for two years, and was soon playing in jazz clubs on Saturday nights in Rennes, the eastern part of France. He was successful, he says, because there was a vogue for the real American "jazz hot." "I was the only black playing music there," he says, and if you were black, "they see that you look like Louis Armstrong." Soon, he quit school and moved to Brussels, Belgium, where he became a full-time musician in clubs and cabarets. "I got married there, and I was playing with everybody. First as a sax player, then as a vibes player, and later on like a bandleader."

By this time, it was 1960 and African nations were gaining independence. It was time to play African music. Since Zaire had been the Belgian Congo, Dibango had made many connections with Zairian musicians in Brussels, and he realized that the first explosion of African music was going to come from Leopoldville. On his arrival, he launched one of the first pan-African hits, the "Leopoldville Twist." "Yes, it was the real twist," he laughs, "the real twist of

Emanuel Bovet

MFA Kera, a versatile vocalist from Senegal, stays in Paris to use modern technology in her experiments with music from an array of sources, including pygmy chants.

Leopoldville: Aye aye aye aye Ooooh." He then joined up with the Grand Kalle and His African Jazz. "He was really number one at the time—along with Franco—and playing with him gave me exposure all over Africa. . . . We did, like, 100 singles, for Africa, only for Africa." He stayed in Kinshasa for two years, opening his own club called the Tam Tam. "And seeing the African landscape, the African atmosphere, made something in my head and I started to compose. But I had not, in my head, a specific style." In addition to the twist and the Congolese rhumba, he recorded jazz numbers and many Latin numbers in Spanish, a style he was well-acquainted with because of the influence from the Santa Isabel period that older Cameroonian musicians had gone through.

Returning to Paris in the mid-60s, Dibango continued recording Congolese music for a while, and then set out on his own. Soul music was popular around the world at the time, and he did some pure rhythm 'n' blues singles, with a sax style that was an homage to King Curtis, the Texan king of the raunchy tenor sax. But Dibango still had what he called his "ethnic side"; for instance, the flip side of a single called "Hot Chicken," an organ-chorded rhythm 'n' blues number of 1969, is a piece with a lot of African percussion. But he still hadn't put the two sides together into his own style.

Meanwhile, in the dance halls of Cameroon, the makossa started to gain strength as a popular dance rhythm. The young musicians of the dance-hall bands were taking the traditional rhythms of southern Cameroon and combining them with highlife and Congolese music. "I was very impressed when I went back to Cameroon and listened to the musicians and saw the people dancing. I mean, this connection between the dance and the music gave me an idea to compose not exactly makossa, but soul makossa, which means a type of vision of the makossa, which is a traditional dance."

Back in Paris again in 1972, Dibango recorded a version of his "Soul Makossa." Coincidentally, that year there were Americans in Paris, scouting out African records for the suddenly booming disco market. "They went to all the labels and took back records and tried it out in the discos in New York and when people started dancing they put it on the radio," Dibango recalls. Soon, "Soul Makossa" was grinding out of every radio and disco speaker in the world. During a night of dancing, an American might notice something different about this particular disco hit, with its flat-toned, multi-layered percussion on the bottom and incessantly repetitive staccato sax line on top. And then there was a deadpan witch doctor's voice repeating "makossa makossa mako makossa" and rapping in an incomprehensible language. But few recognized the number as new African music or as the tip of an iceberg forming in Africa. "After it was a hit, people asked 'What is it? . . . what is it!' "

But Dibango didn't want to be pigeon holed as the makossa man, so instead of explaining what it was, he took the opportunity offered by his success and spent two years in New York playing jazz, jamming with "people I had always dreamed to meet, like Tony Williams, Buster Williams, Frank West, the Brecker Brothers, and this was one of the best periods in my life."

Not that Dibango can avoid soul makossa for very long. At most concerts he has to play some version of it, and now, over thirteen years later, he can hardly turn on an international Top Forties radio station without hearing it. The last minute and seventeen seconds of "Gotta Be Starting Something" on Michael Jackson's mega-hit

Thriller album is "Soul Makossa." "Michael Jackson plagiarized my melody but, after all is said and done, it's a homage to African music," Dibango rationalizes.

Though Dibango hasn't been carried by the current of the success of makossa, he hasn't remained static either. After his stay in New York, he went to Abidjan to lead the prestigious orchestra of the television station there. In doing so, he also took the lead of the music scene of that city in the years when it was becoming the capital of African show business. Since then, Dibango has played every kind of music from free jazz (touring with American Don Cherry, among others) to techno-funk, most recently on the dance single "Abele Dance," and on the album *Electric Africa*, in collaboration with Herbie Hancock. All of his work has a definite African feel to it, but only because he has African material in his musical

New Yorkers feel the beat of Africana All-Stars at the Kitchen.

Keri Pickett

makeup and the skills to record things the way he likes, *not* because he feels an obligation to play African music. "I'm just a musician with a certain background," he says, "like American blacks. But nobody tells them what to play. Maybe if my name was Jackson . . ."

Another Cameroonian who's struggling to be seen as an accomplished musician and avoid being pigeon holed into an ethnic category is singer Bebe Manga. Also from Douala, Manga, like Dibango, was exposed to a wide range of musical influences. Her father played guitar, flute, organ, and accordion, and his favorite songs were "South of the Border, Down Mexico Way" and "Danny Boy." Manga, herself, listened to Elvis Presley and Connie Francis on the "Voice of America" radio show, and she was, of course, exposed to traditional African sounds.

Manga began her own singing career in 1973 in a Douala night-club called La Jungle. There, she was discovered by a Corsican producer and brought to Libreville, Gabon, where, in a club called Au Son des Guitars, she sang French, German, Italian, and English ballads, as well as folk songs from Douala. Finally, she was brought to Abidjan, to another Corsican-owned club called Au Son des Guitars, and there she met her international producer, who brought her to Paris to produce an album. In creating the music for this album, Manga found that she had to reach past her international ballad singing back to her African roots. She came up with a blend of makossa, Congolese, and Western pop that led to the 1982 hit "Ami." "Ami," which was recorded in the Douala language, sold over 1,000,000 copies around the world. Manga toured everywhere from the Caribbean Antilles to Japan. Seven more versions of "Ami" were put out, and Manga received the "Golden Marracas" award in France.

But Manga hasn't put out an album since. She left Paris for New York to pursue a career as an international singing star. "I don't want to be stuck," she says. "In Paris, I know I can get a record contract and I can sell records, but they put you into a category, as African. I want to get out of that whole thing." Her plan is to get an American producer, cut an American album, and return to Paris as an American recording star, therefore "international." But in New York she's been struggling for two years without work, except for an occasional gig with the Brooklyn-based Haitian group Tabou Combo. "I don't know why she won't come back to Paris," says Manu Dibango. "Bebe is a wonderful singer, but there's no structure for her music in New York. Here, she could be putting out records."

A "structure," an organized system of recording, promoting, and distributing records, and an organized way of dividing royalties, is what most musicians feel is lacking in Africa. They also feel it is the

Susan Duane

Bebe Manga, winner of the French "Marraccas D'Or," came to New York to break out of the "African music" category.

Jak Kilby

Opening ceremonies for Stern's African Record Centre in London.

reason that their music is not getting out onto the world market as fast as it could. This need is why many of them have taken up residence in Paris, and, to a lesser extent, Brussels and London. "We're here because of the business system, cosmopolitanism, structure, technology...it's a question of having the equipment, too, and sometimes we say, laughing, that we came to colonize them," says Ismail Toure of Toure Kunda.

Xalam, another group from Senegal that has taken up longtime residence in Paris, stays there because "It's a good time for African music, so we should profit from it," leader Prosper told writer Vivian Goldman. "I've noticed that the media here are ready to accept our music, even more than they are in Senegal. There's 10,000 musics in Africa, you know. Every day people create another new music. But when we stopped playing American-influenced music and started to make a new, more African music, the people in Senegal didn't like the way we used our own traditional rhythms." Xalam is an unusual case because the great amount of jazz influence in their music doesn't fit urban African taste. But self-exile is a common solution for other groups who feel that their local rhythms are either too familiar or too new (in the context of the dance hall) for acceptance by their home market. They feel they must have the added push of acceptance in a foreign market before their music will be welcome back home.

Also, there is certainly more media in Paris to broadcast their music. Besides the Radio France International, which blasts music back to Africa, there are the recently legitimized "underground" stations, such as Radio Gilda, Radio Nova, and Radio Monte Carlo, all of which devote extensive programming time to African music, often back-to-back with other kinds of music from around the world. There is heavy newspaper coverage of events, too; Toure Kunda has been on the front cover of numerous Parisian dailies recently.

Many musicians feel that recording and distribution is easier from Paris, where modern recording facilities are more readily available. "We control production of the records [in Paris]," says Ismail Tonre. "We have a recording company which produces our records and shows, and is, at the moment, pretty strong in the promotion of African music in general. For now, they are fixed on Toure Kunda and Manu Dibango, maybe next will be Youssou N'Dour or Salif Keita or Mory Kante." Most artists feel that they better control the relicensing of their records when they are outside of Africa. Often in Africa a record is licensed to a European company and then the European company relicenses it to other companies without the artist's knowledge or financial participation. Most artists feel that they can monitor this activity better in Paris.

Finally, there is a sense of fraternity among artists in the Parisian scene, and, more specifically, a pan-African unity. Mamadou Konte, who has directed a yearly African festival in Paris since 1978, feels that Paris is the perfect place to reassemble all the black cultures dispersed throughout the globe and to demonstrate their essential unity. "It isn't necessary that the immigrant community is seen as such. The French must understand that the immigrant is not only exoticism. Africa is also in France." His Africa Fete features not only Africans living in Paris, but those from all around the world: North America, England, the Caribbean, and even Africa. Konte has also formed a federation called "la Facen," which helps musicians deal with recording and promotion problems. One of his dreams is the development of an African cultural center in Paris with a restaurant, cinema, and structures for African performances, all coordinated with the governments of the African countries whose performers are involved. This center would also include its own dance troupes and orchestras, and an orientation center for new immigrants. Konte's idea has already been approved by several civic agencies in Paris.

One cultural center for African musicians has already been established. Paco Rabanne, the perfume designer who has a long-time interest in black culture, renovated the old Montgolfier balloon factory on Boulevard de la Villette in Paris, turning it into free rehearsal space for black groups. He's also financing the recordings of several of the groups who have been practicing there since the center's opening in 1983. And there are dozens of Afro-Antillean dance spots in Paris, like the packed Tango, and performance clubs such as New Morning or Chapel des Lombards. These are not located in ghetto areas, but right in the heart of the city's nightclub district. They are frequented by a multiracial clientele.

A similarly well-established African scene exists in London, though on a smaller scale. The city on the Thames has been the home to musicians from Nigeria, Ghana, and South Africa for many years. Fela, for instance, started and operated his Koola Lobitos highlife band there in the early 60s. But London really came into its own as a center for African music in the early 70s, when there was a mini-boom of Afro-rock bands, including Ginger Baker's Airforce, Assagai, and the most successful of the lot, Osibisa.

Osibisa's core musician is a Ghanaian named Teddy Osei. From Kumasi in the Ashanti region, Osei's father played tuba in a church ensemble and was a schoolmaster very interested in traditional music. These musical sparks caught fire for Osei when he had already finished school and was working as a building inspector. In 1958, he formed a highlife band called, first, the Blue Jewels and, then, the Comets, who had a hit song called "Pete Pete" and toured West Africa. But Osei remained a building inspector until 1962, when he went to London to "improve myself either musically or through some other profession." There, he formed highlife groups with other West Africans, played danced at Porchester Hall, rallies for the People's Party of Ghana, and ceremonies for visiting Ghanaian dignitaries. At one of these ceremonies, his sax playing caught the attention of Kwame Nkrumah, and the statesman helped him get a scholarship to the Royal College of Music.

After this study, Osei toured with some success in a group called Catspaw. Returning to London, the group decided to "change the music," according to Osei, "from its essentially highlife orientation to a more refined, internationally acceptable music with strong Afro-roots emphasis." A Grenadan musician, Spartacus R, joined the Africans already involved in the group, now known as Osibisa, which means "criss-cross rhythms." They attracted some attention in clubs and finally landed a contract with MCA Records in 1972. Since that time, they've proclaimed themselves Africa's musical ambassadors as they toured the world. Their most recent triumph was a tour through India.

Other mainstays of the London African scene are Nigerian percussionist Gaspar Lawal and South African Julian Bahula, who was in the group Malombo's original lineup. Lawal played with many British/African groups in the 60s, and then became the most widely employed African session percussionist, working with the Rolling Stones, Airforce, Steven Stills, and Barbra Streisand, among many others. He returned to Nigeria for a roots refresher in 1977 and came back to record his first major album, *Ajomasé*, in 1980. Bahula has been running a nightclub in London called Club 100 and now leads a band called Jabula, who offer a very slick Afro-rock mix.

Other London-based groups—African Connection, Hi-Life International, Orchestra Jazira—continue the tradition of fusing highlife with Afro-Caribbean, Afro-Brazilian, and Afro-American music. Clubs and an active African Center (near Covent Garden) offer performance opportunities for these musicians, along with frequent festivities such as the WOMAD world music festival and 1984's three-week-long African Music Village event in Holland Park, Kensington. But the most important factor that draws African musicians to London are large recording companies—such as Island, Virgin, and Arista, who have been active in releasing crossover LPs—as well as a multitude of independent labels with directors who are enthusiasts of new African pop.

With all this activity, "British Afrophiliacs," writes one of the foremost devotees, Chris May, "have tended to sit around telling each other, with ever-decreasing conviction, that *next* year would be the year African music happened in the UK." He finds, writing in late 1984, though, that optimism for a boom is closer than ever. "It's almost no exaggeration to say," he continues, "that a new local band emerges practically every week."

Unfortunately, many of the problems African musicians face follow them wherever they go. The poor immigrant musician's attraction to the "City of Lights" or the "City on the Thames" may be just as illusory as his attraction to the "City on the Coast" in his own country. Most of the successful transplants seem to have come as students who can afford to wait and let their skills develop for a while before they find work. On the other hand, those musicians who are desperate when they come are bound to be disappointed. There are already enough bands and studio musicians to fill the demand in Paris, and they can't do anything but bide their time and hope for a break.

There are also some new problems for musicians in Paris that don't exist in Africa. Even though instruments are more readily available, they cost a lot of money for someone who has spent most of his savings on the immigration process. And in Paris, it is essential that a musician has his own instrument; it's not like the African system where the bandleader or recording studio provides them. And worse than that, it must be an instrument of competitive quality, which makes it even more expensive.

Working in a European studio also requires some skills not always necessary in its African counterpart. The most important of these is reading music. For better or worse, most African musicians play by ear. "They listen to the record," says Prince Nico Mbarga about his way of teaching new musicians to play his music, "and they have to pick out their own parts." Odion Irnoji, an EMI producer in Nigeria, blames the musicians themselves for not learning this skill, and as a result lessening their possibility for international distribution. "The battle line is drawn between either copying foreign music or developing our own music for the international market. But how can we compete internationally if we can't meet the standards? And how can we develop our music if our musicians don't know their instruments? The majority of session musicians here do not know their instruments. They do not even own their own instruments. And you cannot master an instrument you do not even possess. Okay, instruments are too scarce in [Africa] and they're too costly. But still, [musicians] have money to buy these shoes and silk shirts and stereo radios. The first thing they should buy is a guitar; even a box guitar so they can practice. We have lazy musicians, lazy. They don't work very hard. . . . We also need people who are professional music arrangers....But [if] you bring the music to another country and you use foreign musicians and arrangers, the African element gets weaker and weaker."

Whatever the reason, many African musicians have problems with the multitrack recording process in general. "Africans make lousy session drummers, surprisingly enough," says producer Bob George of Blackmarket Records. "They don't keep a steady rhythm." In other words, they don't keep to the exact rhythm of a synthesized click track; they are used to slightly shifting rhythm, which makes it harder to edit and put together multitrack tapes.

It is difficult to say whether these problems are caused by inept musicianship or by the fact that multitrack recording evolved around Western music, with its rhythmic and harmonic priorities that are very different from those of African music. This may explain why the "African element gets weaker" in the recording process. "You won't get the subtleties of African music on high-tech recordings until Africans themselves master the recording studio the way they've mastered the electric guitar," says Robert Urbanus of Stern's Records in London. Toure Kunda claims they were able to get the exact effects they wanted in recording sessions with New York producer Bill Laswell on their recent *Natalia* LP for Celluloid Records; and King Sunny Adé praised the efforts of producer Martin Messonier in his handling of the difficult task of mixing the talking drums into his Island Album. But some of the most unique aspects of new African pop and African music in general are now often missing from a multitrack recording. Part of the excitement of African music in the suburban Abidjan dance halls, for example, lies in the music's "apart playing," a notion described by musical sociologist John Miller Chernoff as the listener's perception of individual players as independent of each other even though they are all conscious of the same forward motion of time. Chernoff also speaks of the musician's tendency to "push the beat," which is evident in many of the popular dance bands and adds to the drama of the music. These qualities of the music are extremely hard to capture in the recording studio, so are often lost.

But even if the session musician manages to adapt his style to the Parisian recording studio, he will probably encounter other problems similar to those faced by artists in Africa. The standard rates are fairly low, and they become even lower when a producer takes advantage of a musician who just wants to get a foot in the door. "Those official rates are only strictly adhered to by the big celebrities, like Manu Dibango," said a Senegalese percussionist. "Often we have to go much lower for our more unscrupulous compatriots."

Manu Dibango is sympathetic to the problems of young Africans

African music around the world: club goers in Paris.

Emanuel Bovet

trying to become international-class musicians. But he thinks hard work and mastery of modern instruments are a necessary part of the process. "It seems to me that to master our art and to be able to communicate it to others . . . it's necessary to understand a certain number of things. First of all, it's not true that everyone in Africa, in the villages, plays music . . . that it's some sort of natural ability. . . . You must be initiated and believe me, the initiation schools are as rigorous as conservatories. It's necessary to complete the full cycle without which it is impossible to master the music. Mory Kante was sent away for a period of seven years to do this initiation. When a student is able to build his own instrument then, and only then, is he allowed to become acquainted with it. It's hard study that gives the initiate the mastery of his art. It's necessary for young musicians to commit themselves to that sort of discipline. Whatever they choose to do, they must do it the right way, and acquire the technique to best express themselves. . . . To play soccer, you begin by hard training. Music must be practiced also, the talent alone is not enough. What goes for soccer goes equally well for music."

So, in the push to make the music of the modern Africans an integral part of modern world music, the emphasis, for Dibango, Irnoji, and other Africans who have reached international status, is on acquiring the modern skills necessary to express one's personal music style. Not just the skill to be able to copy, but the full mastery that enables a musician to take this technology and transform it into a tool that communicates his own experience.

For example, Paul Wassaba, the musical arranger from Abidjan, feels the key to this communication is a complete knowledge of music notation and theory. Even though he wants to continue using his childhood experience in a Senoufo village as the base of his music, he believes that if he is to develop it, he must be able to communicate his music precisely to other musicians. That's why, though Wassaba is already successful in Abidjan, he's going to study music in the U.S.

Others feel that another key to the communication of African music is the lyrics, since the use of music as a teaching instrument is one of the great characteristics of the African tradition. So, as part of the prescription for the promotion of African music, one African magazine advises: "The international market includes...millions of individuals...who speak French or English. We are inheritors of these two languages, nothing should prevent us from singing in one or the other of them. Africa is able to communicate well from north to south thanks to these two languages. Imagine the lack of them for an instant..." But care must be taken, of course, so that languages are used skillfully enough to convey the desired effect. Fela has managed this with his semi-pidgin declamatory style, using English that suits his music perfectly and gets his point across. Toure Kunda confronts the problem by using a wide palette of languages to suit the music: "With Mandingo," says Ismail Toure, "[we] reach Senegal, Mali, Gambia, the Ivory Coast, Sierra Leone. When [we] speak Peul, [we] reach Cameroon, when [we] sing in French, [we] reach all the French-speaking countries, and when we sing in English, we reach everywhere."

Communication skills in music also allow musicians from various African musical traditions to work together towards a united African musical identity and a united African political identity as well. The political "good times" envisioned by every musician who expresses himself seems to be the era of that unified Africa pleaded for by Kwame Nkrumah. It is seen by many as the only answer to the starvation, corruption, and bloodshed that plague Africa.

To this effect, at the end of 1984 Manu Dibango brought together some thirty of the most famous African musicians and a dozen rhythms to create a "Tam Tam" for Ethiopia, a musical convocation that would result in a record to be sold for the benefit of the starving masses of the Sahel Desert. Among the participants were King Sunny Adé, Salif Keita, Toure Kunda, Mory Kante, and Ghetto Blaster. Everyone wondered what a Mandingo-Wolof-Lingala-Douala-Swahili/Afro-beat-Juju-Makossa-Congolese fusion would sound like. It sounded perfectly natural. With the depth created by a well-equipped recording studio, each performer and each culture proved they had something unique to add to the mix, blended together without losing each individual identity. The high-pitched pleading of Salif Keita, the expressiveness of Sunny Adé's talking drum, the rippling of Mory Kante's kora, the harmonized choruses of Toure Kunda, and the chants of Ghetto Blaster are all recognizable on the record.

These internationally based stars will probably still be seen visiting the dance halls of their home regions to experience the raw excitement of new music in the process of birth. Though this experience is not readily communicable—it's probably one of those things that have to be lived on the spot—it's their job to communicate, so they will transform and combine this music to suit the demands of the world music audience.

But where does this leave the source of all this sound: the traditional music? "Despite the transformations, the innumerable sounds of the city," Manu Dibango once told the magazine *Ivoire Dimanche*, "traditional music lives. I would say that it perpetuates itself. You take a stroll in the evening; you hear people singing—it could be a night guard or a policeman, or even a small boy sitting in front of his family's kiosk. That's how music lives in Africa. It is, in sum, the expression of all the peoples of all the countries. But there's an error here to avoid—that's to think that tradition doesn't change. It adapts itself to each generation. This gives an artist two choices: he can either choose to limit his creativity to his historical past, or he can choose to develop in a way that takes into account his creativity, his past, his present, and his future."

D I S C O G R A P H Y

Various Artists	FLEURS MUSICALES DU CAMEROUN	Socadra Records 3LP
Manu Dibango	SOUL MAKOSSA	CRLP 503
Manu Dibango	ELECTRIC AFRICA	Celluloid 6114
Bebe Manga	AMI	Sono Disc/SIIS 10
Sam Fan Thomas	MAKASSI	Safari Ambiance TAM 4/SA103
Moni Bile	TOUT CA C'EST LA VIE	Safari Ambiance MBO 111
M'Bamina	EXPERIMENTAL	Paco Rabanne 002
Osibisa	CELEBRATION	Celluloid 6703
Gaspar-Lawal	AJOMASE	Cap Records 1
Various Artists	TAM-TAM POUR L'ETHIOPIE	Philips 880 568-1

Ginger Johnson's African Drummers with the Rolling Stones at a memorial for Brian Jones, circa 1969, in Hyde Park, London.

B I B L I O G R A P H Y

Abrahams, Roger D. *African Folktales.* New York: Pantheon Books, 1983.

Andersson, Muff. *Music in the Mix.* Johannesburg: Raven Press, 1981.

Chernoff, John Miller. *African Rhythm and African Sensibility.* Chicago: University of Chicago Press, 1979.

Collins, John. *African Pop Roots.* London: Foulshams Publications, (publication expected Fall, 1985).

Dougier, Henry, ed. *Capitales de la Couleur.* Paris: Autrement Publications, 1984.

Dyan, Brigitte, and Jean-Jaques Mandel. *L'Afrique à Paris.* Paris: Editions Rochevignes, 1984.

Graham, Ronnie. *Stern's Guide to Contemporary African Music.* London: Off the Record Press, (publication expected Fall, 1985).

Jones, A.M. *Studies in African Music.* Oxford: Oxford University Press, 1959.

Moore, Carlos. *Fela Fela: This Bitch of a Life.* London: Allison and Busby, 1982.

Murray, Jocelyn, ed. *Cultural Atlas of Africa.* New York: Facts on File, 1981.

Roberts, John Storm. *Black Music of Two Worlds.* New York: William Morrow and Company, 1974.

Wallis, Roger, and Krister Malm. *Big Sounds from Small Peoples.* London: Constable, 1984.

The following periodicals provide regular coverage on the latest events and releases in contemporary African music:

Africa Music

Tony Amadi International Ltd.
30B Tabley Road
London, N7 ONQ
England

Folk Roots

2 Eastdale, East Street
Farnham, Surrey GU9 7TD
England

Musical Traditions

Westwood Lodge
Rayleigh Road,
Thundersley
Essex, England

New Musical Express

Holborn Publishing Group
5–7 Carnaby Street
London, W1V 1PG
England

The Reggae and African Beat

Bongo Productions
P.O. Box 29820
Los Angeles, California 90029

S O U R C E S

UNITED STATES

African Record Center
1194 Nostrand Avenue
Brooklyn, New York 11225
(718) 493-4500

Largest selection of both imports and their own releases on the Makossa label.

Hannibal Records
Suite 415
611 Broadway
New York, New York 10012
(212) 420-1780

Specializes in Earthworks releases of Southern African music.

Original Music
R.D. 1, Box 190
Lasher Road
Tivoli, New York 12583

Managed by musicologist John Storm Roberts. Well-chosen selection of new African music, plus compilations on Original Music label. Also sells literature.

Rounder Records
One Camp Street
Cambridge, Massachusetts 02140
(617) 354-0700

Selected releases from all regions.

Shanachie Records
Dalebrook Park
Hohokus, New Jersey 07423
(201) 445-5561

Selected releases from all regions.

UNITED KINGDOM

The major retail chains in the U.K., such as Virgin, Our Price, and HMV, have growing African sections.

The following sources specialize in mail order:

Collets
129 Charing Cross Road
London, W1

Earthworks
Unit 30
61–71 Collier Street
London, N1

Gallo Records
Fourth floor
Audrey House, Ely Place
London, EC1

Hot Wacks
60 Daltry Road
Edinburgh, EH11
Scotland

Nomad Records
21 Torbay Court
Clarence Way
London, NW1

Oti Brothers
76 Bedford Hill,
London, SW12

Red Lick Records
P.O. Box 3
Porthmadog, Gwynedd
Wales

Sterns African Records
116D Whitfield Street
London, W1

The other exceptional volumes in the Planet Rock series are:

REGGAE AND LATIN POP:
HOT SAUCES

This illustrative volume traces and illuminates the significance of Latin and West Indian influences in the rich fusions and cross-pollenizations occurring on the current music scene. Covering everything from the tango to the bossa nova, from salsa to reggae and soca, from boogaloo to rock steady, it surveys the backgrounds and musical idiosyncracies of each of the different styles. Among the numerous musicians and groups profiled are Bob Marley, Black Uhuru, Machito, Professor Longhair, Caetano Veloso, Eddie Palmieri, Chano Pozo, and many, many more, with recommendations of the best recordings available, and a plethora of captivating photographs.

EXPERIMENTAL POP:
FRONTIERS OF THE ROCK ERA

Avant-garde musicians have taken amazing strides forward recently, establishing all types of new musical genres and standards, and making their music accessible to a wider audience. Now, EXPERIMENTAL POP will help to fill in any gaps of technology and history and unravel any confusion that may still exist for the listener. It profiles New Music's stars, the groundbreakers who are finally getting the attention they deserve and, in detail, explains their innovative sounds. Philip Glass, Glenn Branca, Meredith Monk, and Laurie Anderson, among many others, are stepping into new musical limelights. This invaluable book, with recommendations of the best recordings, will make sure you are not left in the dark.

ABOUT THE AUTHOR

Billy Bergman, formulator and principal writer for the Planet Rock Series has written on world music fusion in publications from the *EAST VILLAGE EYE,* to the Parisian *AUTREMENT.* Mr. Bergman lives in New York City, where he also writes scripts for short films and multimedia.